HOME BREW

A Guide to Brewing Beer

HOME BREW

A Guide to Brewing Beer

Keith Thomas, Brian Yorston
and Julio Romero Johnson

THE CROWOOD PRESS

First published in 2022 by
The Crowood Press Ltd
Ramsbury, Marlborough
Wiltshire SN8 2HR

enquiries@crowood.com

www.crowood.com

British Library Cataloguing-in-Publication Data
A catalogue record for this book is available from the British Library.

ISBN 978 0 7198 4129 3

Typeset by Jean Cussons Typesetting, Diss, Norfolk
Cover design by Blue Sunflower Creative
Printed and bound in India by Parksons Graphics

CONTENTS

CHAPTER 1

INTRODUCTION TO BREWING BEER

Welcome to *Home Brew: A Guide to Brewing Beer*, a manual that will take you from a basic kit brew to the full production of professional quality beers. Whether your interest is in the technology of brewing, its microbiology, or just the flavours of beer, you will find guidance and examples to direct your brewing activities. A wide range of recipes are provided, covering many different styles, but also as inspiration to draft your own ideas and trials. Home brewing can be a craft activity with a creative element that results in a desirable product. This is a great combination where you can taste the efforts of your labour and enjoy beers of many different characteristics.

Home brewing does have some theoretical background and this guide will outline basic principles and concepts that you can apply to your activities. This will help to develop your knowledge and understanding and allow practical skills to be perfected.

Home brewing today is not a solitary activity, but should be set in the context of a dynamic beer scene of both amateur and commercial producers, illustrating example trends and sharing the areas of expertise involved. Many acclaimed brewers began their brewing at home. As a brewer, you can join the worldwide fraternity of craft brewers, brewing communities and their support networks. This guide will help you to become a creditable brewer – and provide you with some tasteful results to savour along the way.

WHY BE A HOME BREWER?

Answers to the question 'Why are you a home brewer?' often cite the satisfaction of making a product to be proud of. Being able to pour a pint of your own beer is an achievement with many strands of skill, management, judgement and creativity. Moreover, it is a product you can share with family and friends.

As with any craft, there are increasing levels of complexity and technology, but these need not stop a good beer being produced at your first attempt. With time, it is possible to gain experience and knowledge, allowing innovations to develop and a wider range of beers to be achieved, but initially a basic understanding of the process backed up with a simple recipe and instructions will provide the basis for future success.

The counter question is often asked: 'Why are you not a home brewer?', or, more commonly phrased, 'Have you ever tried home brewing?' Common answers are: 'Yes, once, but it tasted so bad I poured it away before anyone else could try it.' Or, perhaps worse, 'Yes, and no one came to my parties again.' Perhaps not so much the last response, but a poor initial experience has certainly stopped many hopeful brewers in their tracks.

This is not because brewing is particularly difficult. Many crafts are more difficult to start, knitting perhaps as an example. However, beer is easily spoilt by some simple mistakes and, most pertinently, is very easily faulted when compared to the commercial brands we regularly drink. One bad home brew becomes a perpetual embarrassment when drinking with friends and family.

Fig. 1.1 An enjoyable taste of a first home brew.

However, a good home brew, appreciated in a suitable social setting, is a subject of pride and acclaim. This is what home brewers aim for and what these pages will support. Like any craft, you are producing something tangible, something you can hold, admire and, of course, taste and savour. It is possible to be both objective and subjective about your creations: objective because you wish to gauge the beer's character against your recipe and expectations; subjective because you wish to enjoy it sensorily.

While bearing in mind personal preferences, it is also good to be aware of the tastes of others with whom you would share your beers. Quite possibly, you will have different preferences and so respond differently to any specific beer. This is perfectly natural; no one wishes to be force-fed a beer they dislike, whatever its acclaim or quality. So, a question to bear in mind is how much will you brew for yourself and how much for friends, family and, possibly, judges in competitions? In many cases, the answer is to brew for all options and, indeed, the mark of a good brewer is to be able to craft a beer to specification, even if it is not to their own taste, or one they would drink regularly.

Drinking your beers regularly is a reward of home brewing – bearing in mind, of course, the need for healthy moderation. Drinking with colleagues, family and friends brings your beers into the social community. Like many craft activities, home brewing has its own communities, both informal and formal. Some are simply having friends taste your beers at home and as part of general sociability. An interesting assessment of this is the assertion that a good beer does not distract from other activities, either by being the focus of praise or an object of concern; it simply becomes part of the activity. At other times, you may savour a beer, or even organize a tasting of a particularly unique brew, perhaps produced for a specific function.

In these cases, commentary is invited and discussion promoted. In an informal setting, you will receive impressions from colleagues, perhaps other home brewers, thereby obtaining valuable feedback on character and quality. It is not hard for informal sessions to become routine if you are brewing regularly and not uncommon to hear of brewing circles developing, with weekly meetings rotating around each other's houses, or even in brew sheds with fully professional dispense and bar-room facilities. (A list of brewing circles and contacts is available in the Appendix.)

Many formal brewing circles have developed in the

Fig. 1.2a   Traditional bar.

BEER & CIDER MENU

	BREWERY	BEER	STYLE	ABV	PINT	HALF
CASK	WENSLEYDALE	FALCONER	GOLDEN BITTER	3.9%	£3	£1.6
	RUDGATE	RUBY MILD	DARK MILD	4.4%	£3	£1.6
	LIVE BREW	V.3.1	OAT & UK HOPPED PALE	4.5%	£3	£1.6
	BRASS CASTLE	BAD KITTY	VANILLA PORTER	5.5%	£4	£2
	DALESIDE	OLD LEGOVER	BEST BITTER	4.1%	£3.5	£1.8
				. %	£	£ .
	KIRKSTALL	THREE SWORDS	EXTRA PALE	4.5%	£3.5	£1.8
		DISSOLUTION	IPA	5.0%	£3.5	£1.8
KEG	SAMUEL SMITH	PURE BREW	ORGANIC LAGER	5.0%	£3.5	£1.8
	SHIPYARD	PORTLAND	US LAGER	4.5%	£3.5	£1.8
	MARSTONS	PEARL JET	NITRO STOUT	4.1%	£3.5	£1.8
	WILD BEER	MODUS OPERANDI	SOUR - OAK AGED OLD ALE	7.0%	£6	£3
CIDER	BROADOAK	MOONSHINE	PERRY	7.5%	£4	£2
	BEARD & SABRE	DOLORES	HOPPED CIDER MEDIUM	4.0%	£4	£2
	KINGSTONE PRESS	APPLE	MEDIUM DRY FIZZY	4.7%	£3	£1.6
	KINGSTONE PRESS	WILD BERRY	SWEET FRUIT FIZZY	4.0%	£3.5	£1.8
				ABV	ML	PRICE
BOTTLES & CANS	SAMUEL SMITH	CHOCOLATE STOUT	←	5.0%	550	£4.5
		OATMEAL STOUT		5.0%	550	£4.5
		CHERRY	FRUIT BEER	5.1%	355	£4
		RASPBERRY	FRUIT BEER	5.1%	355	£4
		YORKSHIRE STINGO	OAK AGED STRONG ALE	8.0%	550	£8
				. %		£ .
	MAGIC ROCK	CANNONBALL	IPA	7.4%	330	£4.2
		SALTY KISS	GOOSEBERRY GOSE	4.1%	330	£3.3
				. %		£ .
				. %		£ .
				5.5%	440	£4.4
	BRASS CASTLE	BAD KITTY ★	VANILLA PORTER	7.5%	440	£5.5
		WALLOP ★	STINGO			£ .
	BAD SEED			4.0%	500	£4
	OLD MOUT	STRAWB. & POMEGRANATE	FRUIT CIDER	4.0%	500	£4
		KIWI & LIME	FRUIT CIDER	0.0%	500	£3
		BERRIES & CHERRIES	ALCOHOL FREE	.		£ .

Fig. 1.2b   Beer listing on a pub menu. Could yours be included?

expertise, evaluating specialist equipment and assessing problems.

At this point, home brewing becomes serious brewing and easily interlinks with commercial brewing. Many successful home brewers have developed into a commercial enterprise, either intentionally as a career choice, or incidentally when asked to supply a local bar. From the authors' experience at Brewlab, this has contributed to the rapid growth of the microbrewery movement. As such, it has generated extensive employment and rewards, particularly in local provision, even if only a few generate extensive financial returns. Be aware, however, that the market for new breweries is increasingly difficult, particularly for wholesale sales. Moreover, being a competent brewer with extensive technical knowledge and skills does not guarantee success. Good business abilities are also essential.

There is a halfway house that has satisfied many home brewers seeking to see their beers in a commercial bar – a collaboration with a licensed outlet. Brewing for a bar, or often a community organization, limits risk while providing opportunity. Many large bars, pubs, tourist venues, museums and so on have function facilities that can provide an outlet for low-volume or occasional brewing. Such

past thirty years, often linked to regional, national or international organizations. These are large enough to organize meetings, competitions and even major technical symposia. Gaining acclaim from such events is a worthy achievement and feedback is always valuable for future improvements. Such circles have further value in arranging bulk purchase of materials, sharing

establishments often have space for production and in-house services of power, water and drainage that can be appropriated. Financial returns may be limited, but the opportunity for getting your beers into the community are often a welcome reward.

Selling beer is, nevertheless, not the primary intent of home brewing and in fact would be illegal without the relevant licences. The main aims are to produce beers you can be proud of, which you enjoy drinking, and to take pride in the skills you have perfected. The chapters that follow will help you to achieve these aims.

BEFORE YOU START: HOME BREWING AND SAFETY

Home brewing is not without its safety issues and these should be taken seriously to avoid any accidents.

Chemicals

Chemicals are needed by the home brewer, either in processing or as a method of keeping equipment clean and sterile. The requirements below should always be followed.

- Use food-grade chemicals when used in brewing and buy them from a reputable home-brew supplier.
- Wear suitable hand and eye protection when handling chemicals.
- Read and follow the manufacturer's instructions before using any chemicals.
- If diluting a chemical, always add the chemical to the water and never the other way round. Chemicals when diluted will give off heat. Adding water to a chemical can cause spitting due to localized heat and steam.
- Never mix chemicals. As an example, bleach and acid will release deadly chlorine.
- Store chemicals away safely – certainly where children cannot reach them.
- Never use caustic soda to clean aluminium pans. The caustic reacts with the aluminium to release explosive hydrogen.
- Rinse away cleaning chemicals after use with clean water.

Heat

You must boil or heat liquids in home brewing, as this not only sterilizes the wort (an important term referring to the liquid produced when the extract is dissolved), but also allows the extraction of malt by the grain brewer and the extraction of the hop bittering compounds. It is a process that cannot be avoided. The requirements below should therefore always be followed.

- Never overfill vessels when heating them up, as boiling wort will produce foam.
- Stand pans on firm surfaces so that there is no opportunity to knock over a pan containing hot liquids.
- When handling hot liquids, wear gloves and keep children away from the activity.

Carbon Dioxide

Carbon dioxide is a by-product of the fermentation process. It is a gas which can asphyxiate and in its pure state is odourless. However, during the fermentation process, the carbon dioxide combines with water and produces a pungent carbonic-acid smell. This can easily be detected in high concentrations. The levels of carbon dioxide produced in the smaller home-brew process are low, but please ensure the following:

- that you have good ventilation when fermenting beer
- that you do not ferment beer near the sleeping area of small pets.

Bottles and Other Containers

Potentially one of the largest issues to the home brewer is the danger of excess build-up of pressure in any beer storage vessels due to secondary fermentation or infection caused by a non-brewing yeast. Too much build-up may cause the container to rupture and if this container is glass it may send dangerous shards in all directions. Yeast will produce carbon dioxide because of fermentation. As a home brewer, you may store your beer in bottles and use the live yeast to carbonate your beer. A separate section of this book will cover how to do this. Here are a few tips to avoid accidents.

- Use the correct container to store your beer. Beer bottles used in home brewing are stronger than those used by commercial brewers, who have greater control of their carbonation process.
- Ensure that all bottles are sound, without cracks or chips, before you fill them.
- A week after filling, check one of your bottles to see if it does indeed have excess carbonation and so warn you that careful handling is needed.
- If one of the bottles of a particular batch has exploded, treat all of that batch as a potential 'bomb' and take the following precautions:
  - handle each bottle as a hazard and wrap it in a towel when moving it
  - wear heavy-duty gloves, a protective heavy jacket and a full-face visor
  - chill down the beer as much as possible, as this will allow the carbon dioxide to dissolve in the beer
  - above a sink or outside in a safe place release the pressure from the bottle, slowly to release the gas. You may have to do this again later, if there is too much pressure.

If you find a flavour fault in the beer, the issue may be caused by contamination rather than excess fermentable sugar. You may want to destroy this beer. Also note that screw- and swing-top bottles have an advantage of failing at the top, rather than the glass shattering.

Electrics
Ensure that any electrical equipment is protected by a circuit breaker and always use a qualified electrician when making repairs and installing new kit.

Alcohol
Please be mindful of the following important aspects of home brewing.

- Alcohol consumption will impair your judgement, so do not to drink when making your beer. Leave this for afterwards.
- Home-brew beer is often stronger than commercial beer. Be aware of this when thinking of using machinery or driving – even on the day after consumption.
- The long-term consequences of drinking are well documented, so please follow government guidelines.

CHAPTER 2

A FIRST BREW

So how can you achieve a successful first brew? Simplicity is the key here, using basic ingredients, a simple brew kit and careful control of hygiene. In fact, hygiene is one of the most common causes of a spoilt beer, so it is vital to develop good hygiene practice from the start and ensure that spoilage is minimized throughout. Safety is another general issue to be aware of while you brew. A list of safety concerns and precautions is detailed in Chapter 1.

Now is not the time to look at the details of brewing biochemistry, engineering or ingredient analysis. These can be assessed later when you can apply them to your increasing knowledge and advanced applications. For now, have a look at a basic malt-extract kit suitable to brew a standard bitter ale.

Later chapters will develop your skills progressively. These will outline a full-grain mash brew using malt and once confident with handling a full brew, you will be able to look at selecting specific malts followed by selecting specific hop varieties. After this, you can try producing specialist beers using different yeast strains and finally more challenging beers, including seasonal ales, herb and fruit beers, and diet beers.

At this point, however, it is important to distinguish what is meant by a malt-extract brew and a full-grain brew. The simplest way to make beer at home is to dissolve some concentrated malt-extract syrup and sugar, add yeast and allow the mixture to ferment into beer. Hops are dissolved in the malt extract so there is no need to boil, although boiling does give a better and longer lasting beer. Malt extract is available from many suppliers as a kit, typically in a 1kg can accompanied by a packet of dried yeast. Not all kits contain hops dissolved in the extract. Some provide a hop extract that can be added, but you also have the option of adding your own hops. Check the

EXTRACT SOURCES FOR BREWING

Yeast needs simple sugars to produce alcohol. In theory, common granulated sugar can be used to produce alcohol, but the yeast will not thrive due to the lack of vital nutrients and the drink will taste quite bland. Traditionally, cereal grains and in particular malted barley are used to make beer, as they provide the sugar for alcohol production and nutrients for yeast growth and of course flavour, body and colour. The advanced home brewer may indeed use grains to brew, but for the novice there are several alternatives.

Malt extract is made by a brewing process using grains. The wort is then concentrated by an evaporation process. When about 80 per cent of the water has been removed, it becomes a thick syrup that can be packaged in a tin ready for the home brewer. This malt-extract syrup can be tailored for a particular beer style, or even to replicate a well-known brand of beer, and can also be already hopped. Dried malt extract, as in Figure 2.1, is further processed from syrup by spray drying until it becomes a fine powder. Extracts eliminate the need to purchase expensive equipment, whilst supplying a well-formulated beer ingredient for the home brewer to use directly as instructed, or even to experiment with.

(continued overleaf)

(continued from page 11)

Fig. 2.1   Dried powdered malt extract.

The grain brewer can use a whole variety of different malts in their recipes and hence produce a much greater range of beers. Other sources of sugars can be found by using different grains such as flaked maize or flaked rice. These are called adjuncts and act as an alternative, often cheaper, source of sugar. Adjuncts are used together with malted barley as this provides enzymes to extract the fermentable sugars from the starch in the adjuncts.

Special brewing sugars can be used and these are tailored for a particular need. Common sugars are invert sugar, which is a mixture of glucose and fructose, and corn or wheat syrups, which can be used to increase the strength of the beer. Brewers' dextrose is simply glucose, but it produces a cleaner, crisper beer. Flavoured sugars provide both extra sugar and a unique flavour. Examples are fruit syrups, molasses, treacle and caramel. This list is virtually inexhaustible as mixtures are possible. Fruit can be used as a sugar source, although the possibility of introducing a non-brewing yeast strain must be taken into account.

The crucial points about these ingredients are that they provide a source of fermentable sugars for the yeast to manufacture alcohol, but they also contribute to beer flavours, either directly through their characteristics, or indirectly via the brewing process.

sidebar on 'Extract Sources for Brewing' for a detailed background.

Full-scale brewing is more complex than kit brewing and involves the following stages:

1. Extracting sugars from malt grains (germinated barley seeds) in a temperature-controlled mash, which digests the grain starch into fermentable sugars.
2. The liquid from this extract (called wort) is then boiled with hops to extract bitterness and flavour.
3. This mixture is then cooled.
4. Finally, it is fermented with yeast. The yeast ferments sugars to ethanol and carbon dioxide, leaving you with beer.

Figure 2.2 shows the stages of the full brewing process, while Figure 2.3 shows how kit brewing differs from this. The sidebars on mashing, boiling and fermentation provide a summary of each of these stages.

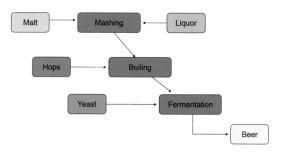

Fig. 2.2   Diagram of stages of the brewing process.

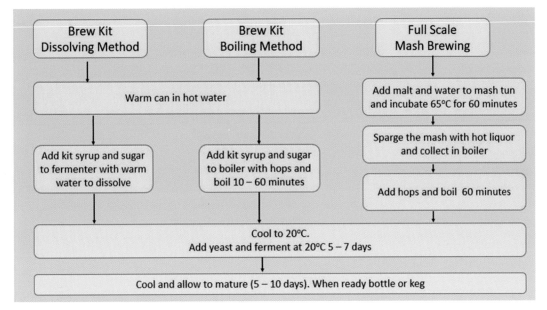

Fig. 2.3   Diagram of kit and mash brewing stages showing differences.

MASHING

Mashing is the heart of brewing, whereby sugars are extracted from the starch in malts. This extraction requires the starch to liquify (gelatinize), to dissolve and then be digested by enzymes into sugars. The mashing process is typically conducted at a temperature that is optimal for enzyme action, generally between 60 and 70°C. The level of acidity and the thickness of the mash are also important factors that the brewer must manage for an efficient extraction of sugars. More extensive details of how to set up and manage a mash are covered in Chapter 3, along with some of the biochemistry and concepts involved.

BOILING

Boiling wort is a process the brewer would rather not do. It is expensive in time and energy, and therefore cost. However, it is vital for several reasons. The boiling process sterilizes the wort and presents a pristine environment for the brewing yeast to be dominant during the subsequent fermentation. It allows the reactions of malt-derived tannins and proteins to form large particles and then be removed from the wort. If these particles were not separated, the beer would eventually go hazy.

The boiling process will evaporate some undesirable flavours. It will also increase the colour, as well as slightly increase acidity. The boiling process is essential for bitterness, as the hop alpha acids are changed to the bitter anti-microbial compound of iso-alpha acid by the process of isomerization. Hop oils and resins are extracted during the boil, although some are lost in the steam.

Therefore, if you did not boil wort, you would produce a hazy, contamination-flavoured beer with no bitterness. The beverage would simply not look, smell or taste of beer.

FERMENTATION

Yeast is a microorganism that can produce energy from sugar using two types of metabolism. In the presence of oxygen, yeast can use a biochemical system called the Krebs cycle, which is common to that used by plants and animals. This system is very efficient in providing energy for life and so allows the yeast to reproduce quickly.

When the oxygen is depleted, an alternative biochemical system called the fermentation process is utilized to generate energy. As a by-product of this fermentation process, both ethanol and carbon dioxide are produced. The fermentation process generates many by-products that have an impact on flavour. Some are desirable, whilst others are not. These include acetaldehyde ('green apples'), diacetyl ('butterscotch') and esters (fruity flavours). The degree of the flavours produced depends on the yeast strain, the wort composition and whether the beer has any contaminant organisms present.

THE STAGES OF BREWING

As can be seen from the diagrams of the brewing process, there are some specific stages as well as some major control steps. Brewing differs considerably from winemaking, in which fermentable sugars are already available in the fruits used. To make wine, it is possible simply to extract the juice, add yeast and manage the fermentation. You can imagine that winemakers will object to this simplification as it ignores many subtle elements of winemaking, but it is valid for comparison purposes.

In your first brew, you will use concentrated malt extract from a pre-prepared wort and so avoid the complexity of the mashing process (this will be encountered in detail later). Instead of mashing grains, a kit will allow you to use malt extract, either as a dried powder or a syrup supplemented with a kilogram of granulated sugar. This will provide much of the fermentable sugars already digested from barley starch. As such, you can simply dissolve the malt extract and sugar into a fermenting vessel and ferment with yeast.

As an alternative, you could choose a kit that requires boiling and add hops. Boiling provides greater stability to beer by reducing possible contamination and so gives

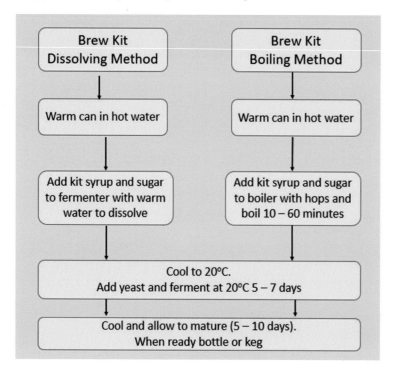

Fig. 2.4   Diagram of brewing processes using basic kit dissolving and boiling processes.

Fig. 2.5 All the materials – malt-extract kit, boiler, fermenter, bottles, tubing, capper.

a longer shelf life, although, of course, you will require a boiler as well as a fermenter. A comparison of the two approaches to kit brewing is shown in Figure 2.5.

This outline of kit brewing provides the basis of brewing, but allows you to make additions in the boil and in fermentation for extra flavours. By using kits initially, you can extend your experience while gaining confidence and skills in managing the operations.

What is Needed for a Basic Brew

Before making a start, some further questions arise. Where should I brew? What equipment will I need? What is the sequence to follow and, equally important, what can go wrong?

Check the illustrations and in the checklist (Table 2.1) for what you will need for a basic initial brew. Most suppliers will carry many options, so look at the listings available. Also check the sidebar on suitable materials for brewing vessels, as some can react with wort and beer.

For this first brew, a simple kit, such as one from the range shown in Figure 2.6, will use prepared malt extract and sugar as the raw materials. Many such home-brew kits are available from suppliers and hardware stores – some use powder, others syrups. All of these contain a stable extract from a cereal mash, sometimes with added hop extract and a packet of powdered yeast.

Fig. 2.6 Example brew kits.

Table 2.1 Essentials Checklist

Materials	Ingredients	Services
Mixing pot/boiler	Beer kit	Water
Kettle and jug	Sugar (generally 1kg)	Power to heat water
Stirrer/long spoon	Detergent	Drainage
Thermometer	Sanitizer	Power to keep fermenter warm
Fermenter		
Bottles and caps		
Tubing and tap		
Capper		

A major starting requirement is a large vessel, generally 25ltr capacity, in order to dissolve and sterilize the malt extract. You can use your fermenter, but a large boiling pan is ideal as you will be able to heat all of the liquid. The type of materials used in brewing vessels is important to consider, partly for expense but also to manage hygiene. Stainless steel is preferred, although plastic is possible. Check details in the sidebar 'Suitable Materials for Brewing Vessels' for further guidance.

The preparation of the wort will take a couple of hours and the fermentation five to seven days. After

SUITABLE MATERIALS FOR BREWING VESSELS

Plastic when used in home brewing has one property that makes it a liability – it tends be stressed by heat and can deform and lose its strength. Therefore, its use for a grain brewer is best limited to the cold side of the operations, such as fermenters and bottles. Plastic can also be weakened by sunlight, as well as being easily scratched and then contaminated by microorganisms.

Fig. 2.7a   Traditional copper brewing vessels.

Fig. 2.7b   Victorian copper fermenter.

Historically, copper was universally used in breweries, as it was the only metal available. It is an excellent conductor of heat and is wettable, so causing small bubbles that help in trub formation. This makes it ideal in areas such as wort kettles using direct heat transfer. The disadvantages of copper are its excessive cost and that it is relatively soft, so is liable to scratches and dints. It will leach copper ions into the wort, which can be beneficial to remove sulphur compounds and supply small amounts of copper for the yeast growth. However, excess copper (above 0.2mg/ltr) can be toxic to humans. Copper tarnishes easily, so needs constant cleaning using acids to keep its inherent beautiful colour.

Today, the material of choice is stainless steel. It conducts heat, is strong, durable to cleaning chemicals and does not tarnish. It is easily cleaned and does not taint the product. Although invented in the 1800s, it was not until the 1950s that it became economically viable to use. Stainless steels are an alloy of iron, chromium and nickel. Two types are used in brewing. Type 304 has a composition that includes 18 per cent chromium and 9 per cent

nickel. Type 316 has the addition of 2 per cent molybdenum. Type 316 is superior and so more expensive, as it provides greater resistance to acids and corrosion by chloride ions.

Brass, iron and aluminium should be avoided at all costs in brewing, as they may leach metals into the beer. Brass contains small amount of lead, which under acidic conditions can end up in beer. Iron will cause beer flavour and haze issues, whilst aluminium in contact with caustic soda will react to produce explosive hydrogen and dissolve away your vessel. Aluminium coated with an intact inert coating can be used, although is not ideal as the coating may deteriorate.

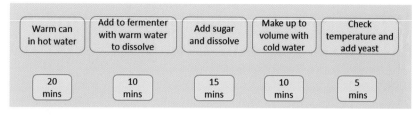

Fig. 2.8a   Timings of dissolving – boiling.

Warm can in hot water	Add to fermenter with warm water to dissolve	Add sugar and dissolve	Make up to volume with cold water	Check temperature and add yeast
20 mins	10 mins	15 mins	10 mins	5 mins

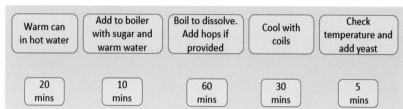

Fig. 2.8b   Timings of dissolving – method kit brews.

Warm can in hot water	Add to boiler with sugar and warm water	Boil to dissolve. Add hops if provided	Cool with coils	Check temperature and add yeast
20 mins	10 mins	60 mins	30 mins	5 mins

this, the beer requires checking before bottling to be sure it is stable. Once bottled, your beer should ferment slowly as it matures for a further seven to ten days. This will generate carbon dioxide in the bottle and the beer will become conditioned and effervescent when opened. After this, your beer is ready for you to taste.

To view how long your brew will take, check with the flow schemes in Figures 2.8a and b showing the example timings of basic no boil and boiling options.

GETTING STARTED

So, to get started have a look at the preparations needed – and the questions to check in advance.

Space

First, you need a suitable space in which to work, most likely a kitchen. Even brew kits require the liquid to be heated, in order to dissolve the malt extract powder or syrup. Either of these will be sticky once opened. They are easily spilt, so a clean and wipeable surface is essential. You don't want the extract getting into corners or in the cracks of tables and floors, as this will encourage microbes to grow and potentially spoil your beer. You also don't want complaints from other kitchen users. A standard laminate kitchen worktop is ideal, although this could be situated in a clean shed, workroom or garage.

Easy access to a sink and water supply is also vital, as you will need to wash your vessels and utensils. You will

also need power to heat and dissolve the wort and a means to cool it before adding yeast. Again, a kitchen is a suitable location for these, but it is worth considering the options available in some detail

Fig. 2.9a   Suitable brewing location with services – worktop.

Fig. 2.9b   Another brewing location – sink surface.

Water

Water will be the major ingredient in your brew. Often termed liquor by brewers, your water supply needs to be potable (acceptable for drinking). To make it safe and potable, suppliers typically treat water with chlorine – which you can often smell when the tap is running hard. This chlorine is bad news for your brew. Being quite reactive, it readily combines with wort and beer components, producing medicinal off flavours. As a result, it is a sad cause of many rejected beers and a common home-brew fault.

To avoid this, it is sensible to boil the water before starting and leave it standing for some time to cool – for a few hours or overnight – before mixing it with your extract. An alternative is to add Campden tablets

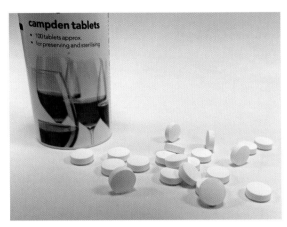

Fig. 2.10 Campden tablets to remove chlorine from the liquor.

LIQUOR OR WATER SOURCES

It can be argued that water, or liquor as termed by brewers, is the main ingredient in beer – beer consists of about 94 per cent water. Sourcing a good water supply is therefore vital for the manufacture of good beer. In most cases, it will come straight from your domestic tap. By law, this is guaranteed by your utility company to be wholesome. There are some issues with tap water, however, as it is often treated with chlorine or chloramine to prevent bacterial contamination. These chemicals can cause beer to have a TCP (trichlorophenol) or medicinal taste. If you want to avoid TCP and medicinal flavour problems:

- Buy your brewing water in a bottle. Although more expensive, it will be guaranteed chlorine or chloramine free. It will also list the mineral content.
- Boil your liquor for at least 15 minutes and cool. This will drive off the chlorine, but not any chloramine.
- Filter your water through either an activated carbon or a reverse osmosis filter.
- Add Campden powder as a tablet as in Figure 2.10, following the instructions provided. This will remove both chlorine and chloramine.

For the grain brewer, there is an added dimension in that salts have an influence on the extraction of sugars from the grain. The balance of salts has a huge effect on beer flavour and is linked to beer styles. Therefore, an understanding of the levels of different salts in your water supply and the treatment needed for different beer styles is paramount. The notable salts in brewing are calcium sulphate, calcium chloride and bicarbonates. This is not an issue for the extract brewer.

You may be tempted to use rainwater as a brewing source, as it would have no salts, in theory making their addition easier, as you would be starting from a blank canvas. However, please do not use rainwater, as it may contain harmful contaminants picked up from the environment. The same applies to well or river water, which could be high in undesirable materials such as iron, nitrates, heavy metals or pesticides. The price of domestic water in the UK is a minor cost to the home brewer and well worth using as an insurance to produce good beer.

(sodium or potassium metabisulphite), which react with the chlorine. Half a tablet will treat 22.7ltr (5gal), but ensure you grind up the tablet so that it dissolves fully.

The sidebar on 'Liquor or Water Sources' provides a summary of the features and different sources of brewing water.

Power

Wort also needs to boil – or at least be heated. This is partly to dissolve the sugars and other ingredients, but also to kill off microbes and to sterilize it. In fact, it is impossible to kill off all microbes for certain by boiling, though you can get pretty close after 10 minutes at 100°C.

Electricity and gas are the most common heating sources in kitchens, so if you choose a kit to boil wort you will need a metal vessel to hold this as it heats. Stainless steel is a good material, being inert and hygienic, and aluminium undesirable. The ideal vessel is one designed for brewing with a tap for the run-off, so that you don't have to lift a heavy or hot batch of wort to pour into your fermenter. If you can afford it, purchase a dedicated brewing boiler, which will have an internal electric heating element, generally 2–4kW, which you can plug into a mains supply (*see* Figure 2.9a). Figure 2.11 shows the internal heating element in a boiler.

Alternatively, a large, solid pot will suffice if it is stable on a cooker ring (either electrical or gas), as in Figure 2.12. An induction ring is ideal, if your pot is

Fig. 2.12   Boiling with gas.

suitable. Safety is an issue here, as you may need to move the pot when hot, so make sure that any pot has solid, and well-insulated, handles.

Cooling

Boiled wort must be cooled before the yeast is added for fermentation. This will of course happen naturally over time – certainly overnight. However, leaving the hot, but cooling, wort for an extended time may encourage oxygenation, leading to stale flavours – another common home-brew fault. If you choose this approach, transfer your wort to a container with a sealable top so that it can cool hygienically.

Forced cooling can be achieved by sitting the boiling pot in cold water. Early home brewers used to stand the pot in a filled bath for hours, inevitably leading to

Fig. 2.11   Boiler with heating element and mesh to retain hops.

Fig. 2.13   Cooling coils suitable for rapidly chilling the wort.

conflict with other bathroom users – a further home-brew fault. An easier option is to insert a cooling coil (*see* Figure 2.13) into the wort and run cold water through the coil to remove the heat. Stainless-steel or copper pipe is the most effective for this, as shown in the diagram, and can cool a 25ltr batch of wort within 20 minutes.

One difficulty with a cooling coil is the connection to taps, which in a domestic kitchen lack screw fittings. Garden-hose connectors are available that can overcome this, but check your taps carefully to ensure a tight joint and avoid water spraying around the room – a very undesirable home-brew fault.

Utensils

Steady, confident hands are essential to manage your home brew and avoid spillages. However, a few utensils are worth purloining. A large, solid spoon at least 45cm long is good to remove syrup from a tin and to stir the wort. Stainless steel or plastic is probably better than wood, which can harbour microbes.

A thermometer is desirable to check the temperature of the wort before adding the yeast. A weighing balance is useful if you need to weigh any additional ingredients (*see* the recipe advice for options). Some tubing is desirable to transfer beer from the fermenter to bottles or a beer keg. Tubing is typically PVC due to

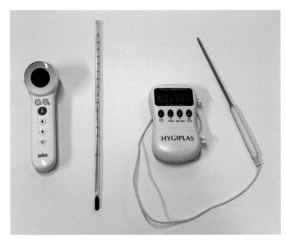

Fig. 2.15   Spirit, digital and surface thermometers suitable to monitor your brewing.

its flexibility, but must be food grade otherwise plastic taints may leak into the beer. It is also important to sanitize tubing thoroughly, as it will easily harbour contaminants on its internal surfaces.

Monitoring Equipment

A standard liquid thermometer will suffice for general use, but must be spirit and not mercury due to toxic contamination if broken. Digital thermometers with an immersion probe are valid, but check the accuracy when you select. Some options are shown in Figure 2.15. Ideally, an accuracy of +/– 0.5°C is desirable, particularly for mash brewing, but +/–0.2°C would be even better for consistency control. Remote pointing surface thermometers, such as used for fever monitoring, are also worth considering if you can source one with a suitable range (0–100°C), as this will reduce your exposure to scalding-hot steam.

Weighing Balance

With a brew kit this is not essential as the ingredients will be pre-prepared. If you are supplementing your kit brews, look for a balance like the one in Figure 2.14 to measure to 1g or even 0.1g units, as you may need to add small amounts of hops, which are full of flavour and very light.

If you are looking to keep a minute-by-minute check on your fermentation, you may consider a Wi-Fi

Fig. 2.14   Basic equipment – spoon, thermometer and balance.

Fig. 2.16 Weighing balance with scale display.

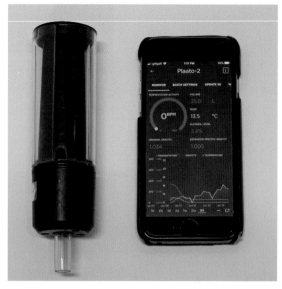

Fig. 2.17 Automatic logging airlock with phone display.

gas-flow monitor (*see* in Figure 2.17). These measure the amount of carbon dioxide released through an airlock and relay this to your mobile app, showing you fermentation progress and allowing you to judge temperature control. Although relatively expensive, these do allow you to have a brew in your pocket.

An Essential Word on Hygiene

What is the cause of most spoilt beer? Microbial contamination. And why? Because of poor hygiene.

Beer is not the easiest liquid for microbes to colonize, for example when compared to milk or meat. It is acidic and contains alcohol and hops – all of which inhibit bacteria and yeast. It also lacks oxygen when

fermented, which limits mould growth. However, there are some very specific microbes that have adapted to growing in wort and beer, particularly the lactic-acid bacteria, the acetic-acid bacteria and wild yeasts, as shown in Figures 2.18a, b & c respectively, which will cloud your beer and produce undesirable flavours.

All of these microbes are present in many environments, such as soil, plants, food, dirt, on animals and, of course, on ourselves. Microbes are difficult

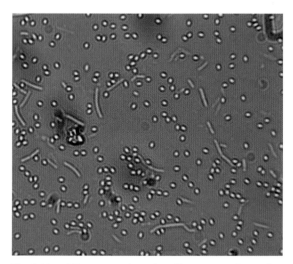

Fig. 2.18a Microscope view of spoilage contaminants in beer – lactic-acid bacteria.

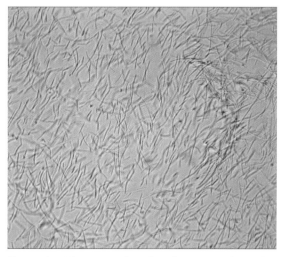

Fig. 2.18b Microscope view of spoilage contaminants in beer – acetic-acid bacteria.

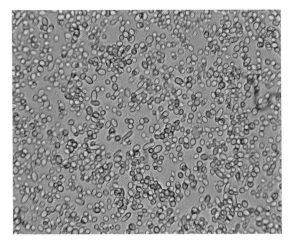

Fig. 2.18c Microscope view of spoilage contaminants in beer – wild yeast.

Fig. 2.19 Wort spillage providing flies with a nutritious feed.

to see without a microscope, but they are present in the air, on surfaces (including hands) and in liquids, particularly those left exposed for any length of time. As a result, you need protect your wort and beer where you can. All surfaces in contact with wort and beer should be cleaned and sanitized, including washing hands well before starting. It is equally essential to clean surfaces when you are finished, as spills of wort and beer and dust from malt rapidly become contaminated with microbes, as shown in Figure 2.19. Wort and beer also attract flies, which are experts at getting into your fermentation and transmitting contaminants.

Cleaning and sanitizing are two different processes. Cleaning uses detergents to dissolve soil from surfaces, but does not necessarily remove or kill microbes. Sanitization uses sterilizing chemicals to

kill microbes, and so leaves the surface ready for use. However, sanitizers do not work well if the microbes are surrounded with soil on poorly cleaned surfaces. Cleaning and sanitization should be applied in sequence to be sure that you have hygienic conditions. Figure 2.20 shows this sequence. As cleaners and sanitizers can react together, it is important to rinse surfaces between cleaning and sanitizing and at the end of sanitizing unless a food-compatible sanitizer has been used.

Your brewing location thus needs to limit the presence of microbes by having clean surfaces, and by not having open foods exposed, for example milk products, old vegetables or fruits, or open compost or rubbish bins. Swabbing surfaces to clean and sanitize will reduce the aerosols being generated, and, while you won't need to wear a lab coat, you certainly don't want to wear gardening kit.

Home-Brew Kit Instructions
So, if you are now all prepared, following is the procedure for producing a beer from a brew kit.

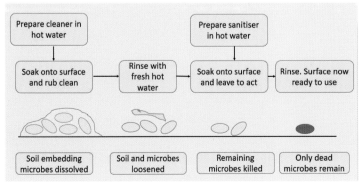

Fig. 2.20 The cleaning sequence showing removal of soil and sterilization of surfaces.

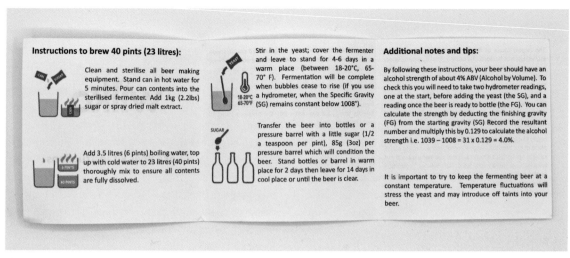

Fig. 2.21   Example kit instructions for dissolving malt syrup.

First, check the kit instructions. Most beer kits today are based on syrups, generally concentrated wort from a large brew. If you have a syrup kit, usually in a can, it may be advisable to warm the can in a bowl of warm water so that the syrup flows easily. If you have a powder kit, handle carefully to avoid releasing clouds of the powder into the atmosphere. It will easily make you cough – and make everything around sticky. Ideally wear a mask, particularly if you are asthmatic. Figure 2.21 shows some typical instructions from a syrup kit.

The procedure for such kit beers is basically to dissolve the extract and extra sugar in the appropriate amount of hot water and allow the mixture to cool, as shown in Figure 2.21 above. Finally, add the yeast and leave in a warm place to ferment. This generally takes a week or so, after which you can mature the beer for a few more days, then bottle or transfer it to a conditioning keg from which you can dispense draught beer.

BREW DAY

On your chosen brew day, you will need the kit materials, the equipment specified above and space and time in which to conduct the process. Assistance can be useful, but beware of too many brewers in a small space crowding out your kitchen.

The target for the brew day is to dissolve the kit

Fig. 2.22a   Dissolving the extract.

Fig. 2.22b   Stirring to dissolve the extract.

components into a set volume of water and inoculate with yeast, while avoiding contamination throughout. As mentioned previously, with many kits you can add 3–4ltr of boiling water to the fermenter to dissolve the malt extract and sugar (*see* Figures 2.22a and b). Stir well to ensure that the malt-extract syrup and sugar are dissolved, then make up to volume with cold water. This option is relatively easy, but runs some risks because of the chlorine in the cold water, so consider using a Campden tablet to neutralize the chlorine. This procedure is suitable for those kits that have all ingredients except sugar together – malt extract, hop extract and any yeast nutrients.

In other kits, you are encouraged to add the extract and sugar to a larger volume, then to boil. There is likely to be less contamination, but it does require managing a vessel of boiling wort, as in Figure 2.23. If you are adding whole hops or pellets, it will be necessary to boil to extract the bitterness and aroma. The kit will specify the volume of water required, which can be heated up in the boiling pot. Here, safety needs reiterating. If heating on a stove, ensure that the pot is balanced and can't easily topple over. Work near a sink in case of spills and splashes and keep children and pets well away.

Those kits that contain separate ingredients – malt extract, hop cones or pellets and yeast – allow some flexibility with processing, as the bitterness and hop aroma depend on when the hop pellets are added to the boil, or afterwards to the beer. Generally, the instructions will guide you to make the best choice, but there is no harm testing your own conditions. Have a look at the example instructions in Figure 2.24 from a typical kit and their directions on using the kit as the basis for boiling your brew.

One critical feature of mixing your ingredients is the temperature of the wort before you pitch the yeast. This should be in the range 19–23°C for ale yeast and 10–13°C for lager yeasts. A little higher will have limited effect, as long as you manage the fermentation temperature (as discussed later). However, if your wort remains over 25°C, the fermentation may be abnormal and generate undesirable flavours. If the wort remains nearer 35°C, there is a chance you will kill many of the yeasts and have no fermentation at all! Alternatively, if you add yeast to cold wort the fermentation will take longer, but beware not to have the wort below the recommended temperatures noted above, as the fermentation will be slow or stop entirely.

Fig. 2.23 Boiling wort to extract bitterness from hops.

Fig. 2.24 Example commentary from boiling kit instructions.

ADDITIONAL FLAVOURS

Many unusual flavour ingredients can be used in brewing. Here are just four that have a clear impact on flavour and are easily sourced. As with all ingredients, remove any parts showing decay. A brief scald in boiling water can remove external contaminants and preservatives that may affect fermentation.

Ginger

Ginger beer can be made either as a soft drink, or fermented to produce an alcoholic version. The flavours produced by ginger are fiery and aromatic. The manufacture of ginger beer uses sucrose as the fermentable sugar, together with lemon juice to enhance the ginger note. When using ginger in a malt beer, some of the ginger characteristics are masked by other flavours such as hops. You can use ginger roots or the powdered version, but it is best to add these to the kettle during the boil to extract the ginger and to ensure that no microbiological contamination finds its way to the fermenter. Ginger essence can be used for adjustment post-fermentation to suit the flavour you require.

Coriander

Coriander has been used in beer since medieval times, including in some present-day Belgian beers. The seed of the coriander is used and is best added to the wort at the end of the boil. It has compounds like those found in hops and when used in beer gives a pleasant fruity citrus flavour.

Liquorice

Liquorice tends to be used in dark beers. It imparts fennel, aniseed or star-anise flavours into beer. It is a woody root that can be dried and cut into sticks. This root can be added directly to the kettle at the end of the boil to extract the goodness. Shredding the root will enhance the extraction process. Liquorice can be bought as a concentrate, powder or stick. Liquorice does contain a poison, glycyrrhizin, which at high concentrations can cause human health issues, so be cautious with additions.

Chilli

The heat of the chilli is caused by capsaicin and the amount of capsaicin in each pepper is measured on the Scoville Scale. Different types of chilli peppers will give varying amounts of heat, so be aware of what type you are using and its effects. Addition of chillies can be made in the kettle to avoid contamination by microorganisms. One way to control both the issues of too much heat and any contamination is to boil up a liquor of chillies. Add the resultant extract carefully to the fermented beer to assess the heat contribution. This will tell you precisely how much extract to add. Some brewers have been known to add a whole chilli to a bottle of beer for visual effect, but beware of a hot mouthful!

Fig. 2.25   Additional ingredients to try – ginger, chilli, coriander and liquorice.

To minimize contamination when adding the yeast, open it just before with clean hands and avoiding anything else falling in. Most packets of yeast today are prepared for direct addition to the wort, although some benefit from a brief recovery in warm water (around 30–35°C) before pitching. Check instructions to avoid problems. Also be aware that stronger brews – those with high sugar levels over 1.040/1.050 specific gravity – require a higher concentration of yeast than standard brews. Brews using lager yeast also require a higher pitch of yeast, potentially twice as much as ale brews, as they ferment more slowly. When brewing kit beer your yeast provision should match the wort, so if you make additions such as extra sugar it is advisable to adjust your yeast.

While kits are tested to make good beer of the style specified, they do allow you to add other ingredients. Additional malt may be added to provide more alcohol – within limits. More sugar will do the same – again within limits. Be aware, particularly when adding purified sugar (glucose and sucrose) to extract brews that it may disturb the yeast metabolism and produce off flavours. You can,

though, substitute other sugars for simple granulated sugar, for example brown sugar, demerara, or even honey or the specialist candi sugar used in Belgian beers.

Flavourings are more interesting additions to consider. Simple spices such as ginger, coriander, liquorice, chilli and fruits are common options, but invention and mixtures offer wide scope to vary your brew. Further details are included in the sidebar 'Additional Flavours'.

At the end of the brew day, you will have prepared the wort, inoculated it with yeast and placed it in a suitably warm location for fermentation. To prevent contamination with undesirable microorganisms, your fermenter should have a loose-fitting lid, or an airlock attached, as in Figure 2.26. As a considerable volume of carbon dioxide will be produced, ensure that your fermenter is not tightly sealed. You do not want your beer to end up exploding.

Finally, and remembering to maintain good hygiene, you will also have cleaned everything ready for the next brew and, quite possibly, opened a beer to anticipate what will be produced.

AFTER THE BREW – FERMENTATION

The next step is the productive phase of brewing – fermentation. For this stage, you will need controlled attention but minimal disturbance. Fermentation takes time and depends critically on temperature. Too low a temperature, particularly for ale yeast, and it will stop. Too high and your beer will be unbalanced due to the wrong flavours developing. A good range of temperatures is 19–23°C for

Fig. 2.26   Example basic fermenter and conical fermenter with temperature control.

ale yeast and 10–13°C for lager yeasts. Managing this is not easy, particularly in winter when heating falls during the night. Ideally, look to collect the wort in your fermenter around these temperatures. During active fermentation the yeast will generate heat.

However, when fermentation is beginning is a critical period, during which the yeast may fail to start working if kept too cold. Insulating your fermenter is one solution; applying thermostatically controlled heating through a heat pad or brew belt is another. Constructing an incubator for the fermenter is often undertaken by the serious brewer, while purchasing a fermenter with inbuilt temperature control, such as in Figure 2.27, is an option for brewers with an investment of up to £1,000.

In large fermentations, say over 100ltr, the heat generated by active fermentation is a problem as the beer may overheat, so causing flavour defects. In these cases, generally in commercial brewing, chilling is needed, often through jackets surrounding the fermenter, or through cooling coils within the beer. On smaller-scale production, below 100ltr, the heat generated is typically lost to the surroundings and the beer cools down. Insulation or temperature control is essential. At suitable temperatures, fermentation will take three to five days for a standard recipe producing 4–5%ABV (Alcohol by Volume) beer. Longer may be necessary for stronger beers and up to fourteen days for lagers due to their low-temperature fermentations.

Fig. 2.27 Temperature-controlled fermenter with airlock.

During fermentation, the sugars in the wort will be converted by the yeast into alcohol and carbon dioxide, with a side order of flavours at lower concentrations. The alcohol mostly stays in the beer, but the carbon dioxide progressively effuses from the beer. You will easily see this release of carbon dioxide if there is an airlock attached, as bubbles of gas float through the liquid and can be heard popping into the atmosphere.

Tasting the beer through this period will confirm that the sweetness declines, allowing bitterness to be more noticeable. Fruity flavours and, possibly, sulphur and spicy flavours may also increase. The beer will also become more turbid and cloudier.

Towards the end of fermentation, the beer will show less gas release and eventually clears as the sugars become used up and the yeast settles (flocculation). Normally, it is advisable to leave the beer for some days after the end of fermentation until it is clear enough to package, and then chill it to accelerate this. Commercially, this would be down to 0°C, but in home-brew conditions 10°C would be a good target. Moving your fermenter into an unheated room in winter should achieve this, but in summer (always a difficult brewing season) you may need a chilling system, or perhaps a converted fridge.

A critical feature at this stage is how to know when the beer has finished its fermentation. To some extent, this will be evident from a reduction or cessation of bubbles through the airlock and the thickening of the yeast head on the top of the beer. At this point, it is relevant to consider some valuable technology to assist your judgement – the saccharometer.

Measuring Gravity – the Saccharometer

A little background. A valuable measure of fermentation is the amount of sugar present in the wort initially and in the beer as it ferments. The level of sugar present will gradually reduce as it is fermented into alcohol and carbon dioxide. An easy measure of the fermentation is to test the sugar present using a saccharometer – in effect, a hydrometer calibrated for sugar concentrations. This indicates the density of the liquid that declines as the sugar is fermented.

The saccharometer is a weighted glass (or plastic) cylinder that floats in the wort or beer. Saccharometers have a long stem with graduations calibrated against sugar concentrations and are available in different sizes (*see* Figure 2.28a). In water, the saccharometer will float with a graduation of 1.000 – the comparative density against other solutions (*see* Figure 2.28b). Sugar solutions will have a higher reading as they are denser than water. The saccharometer readings are referred

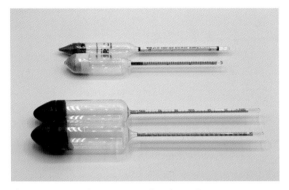

Fig. 2.28a   Saccharometers of various sizes.

Fig. 2.28b   Floating in wort to show gravity measurement.

to as the specific gravity. For most beers of a 4–5%ABV, the original gravity of the wort before fermentation will be between 1.040 and 1.050.

Standard brewing worts will have a range of sugars present, predominantly glucose, maltose and maltotriose as fermentable sugars, as well as more complex unfermentable dextrin sugars. At the end of fermentation, the beer should just be left with the dextrins, which the yeast cannot use. At this point, the beer is ready to bottle or keg.

One major complication is that the beer needs some additional fermentation in the bottle or keg to produce a fizz of carbon dioxide and make the beer sparkle on the tongue. To achieve this, it is necessary either to add some additional sugar (the easiest option), or to package the beer while a small amount of sugars remain (less intrusive, but often difficult to judge).

For your first brew, take the easiest approach and allow the fermentation to complete until only the dextrins are left and then add some sugar when the beer is bottled or kegged. To prevent over-carbonation and possible bottle explosion (a further, and dangerous, home-brew fault), you should leave the beer to mature fully and ensure that there is no fermentation to complete. You need to be absolutely sure, however, that there are no residual sugars left, for example if the fermentation stopped midway due to a cold spell, as these may re-ferment as the bottle warms up.

To check the extent of the fermentation, measure the specific gravity. As the concentration of the unfermentable dextrins is typically 20–25%, you will be looking for the final gravity to be 20–25% of the original gravity. As you are making a 4.0%ABV beer, the gravity when fermentation is complete will be around 1.010 (remembering it started at around 1.040). If the beer gravity remains the same for a few days, it should have completed the fermentation.

AFTER THE BREW – MATURATION

Although your beer has completed its fermentation, it may not be fully ready to package. Some maturation time may be needed to balance flavours. This depends on style and strength and requires some experience to judge. In general terms, five to seven days is a desirable maturation for standard and low to moderate strength beers (below 5%ABV). Ten to fourteen days may be desirable for stronger and darker beers. During this time, keep your beer cool and undisturbed so that there is limited chance of contamination and spoilage.

Some maturation will occur in the bottle and you may find that an earlier bottling allows this to develop. Again, experience will provide guidance.

AFTER THE BREW – PACKAGING

Once your beer has matured for a time after fermentation it should be clear enough to package – either into a keg or bottles. Both methods have different potentials and disadvantages, so a look at the options in Table 2.2 will help you decide.

At this stage, it is worth addressing the hazards prevalent in packaging. Two are particularly evident – hygiene and carbonation. A subsidiary hazard is oxidation. All of these make packaging a complex part of the process.

The issue of hygiene was covered earlier, but applying it to packaging requires careful attention, as the beer is particularly vulnerable to microorganisms both from the air and from utensils. Whatever your choice of packaging, the beer must be transferred

Fig. 2.29   Racking beer from a fermenter.

from the fermenter, either directly from a tap or by syphoning through some tubing. The need for tubing to be clean has been stressed already, but as a further precaution it is advisable to soak tubing in boiling water just before use.

Depending on the design of your fermenter, there will most probably be a tap of some sort through which to draw the beer. Tubing may be coupled to a tap, or you may be able to draw the beer directly from the tap straight into the keg or bottles. Using a jug is a possibility, but increases the potential of contamination, as does syphoning through tubing. If using tubing, a syphon may need to be developed (*see* point 6 below) in order to draw the beer out of a

Table 2.2   Listing of Brew Keg- and Bottle-Filling Features

	Brew Keg	Bottle
Volume (typical)	10–20ltr	330–500ml
Materials	Generally plastic, possibly stainless steel	Glass
		Must be reusable strength if refilling
Ease of fill	Easy in one run	Needs repeat fills
Sealing	Generally has a screw thread, but take care as may leak	Caps are generally tight if using suitable capper
Shelf life of 4–5%ABV beer	Can be limited – weeks	Can be extensive – months
Ease of dispense	Requires tap or pipework to a font	Easy by bottle opener
Hygiene	Progressively difficult with age if plastic due to abrasions on surfaces	Easy to clean manually and chemically

SUGAR CALCULATIONS

Adding the correct amount of sugar to prime your keg or bottle is a critical judgement. The following provides some guidance and background.

By the stoichiometry of fermentation reactions, 0.7g per litre of sugar will produce 1g per litre of CO_2. By calculation $0.7 \times 4 = 2.8$g per litre of sugar is needed to achieve 4g per litre of CO_2 noted earlier. For a 500ml (0.5ltr) bottle, we thus need 1.4g. For a 20ltr brew keg, we will need $2.8 \times 20 = 56$g. Sugar solutions encourage microbial growth, so prepare these just before you bottle and not the day before.

The easiest approach is thus to dissolve sugar at a suitable concentration and add the right amount to each bottle or keg. A suitable solution would be one containing 1.4g in 5ml, as this volume is relatively easy to measure using a pipette or measuring spoon. If you have brewed 20ltr you would thus dissolve 56g in 200ml of boiling water. Once dissolved, allow to cool and add 5ml (around a teaspoonful) to each bottle, or add all 200ml to a 20ltr brew keg.

Fig. 2.30   Getting the right measure: 2g of sucrose in a spoon.

of very strong sugar syrup that can kill or inhibit the yeast from further fermentation. A better solution is to dissolve the sugar before adding – that is, to make a solution of sugar in boiled water. Ideally, most beers need to be moderately fizzy, which translates to around 4g of carbon dioxide per litre, or 2g for a 500ml bottle. More details on the calculation of sugar additions are available in the sidebar 'Sugar Calculations'.

The Packaging Day

As with your brew day, the packaging session needs a clean environment and careful attention. Here is a suggested sequence of operation using the system shown in Figure 2.31.

1.   Prepare and clean the materials needed, including bottles and/or brew keg.
2.   Carefully position the beer so as to be easily accessible. Avoid any major disturbance when you move the fermenter, as this will re-suspend the yeast and give you cloudy beer. It is helpful to have the fermenter a metre or so off the floor, so that you have some height above the bottle fill level.
3.   If drawing beer through a tap on the fermenter, clean and sanitize the external tap surfaces, for example with some hot water ($>65°C$).
4.   Sanitize the bottles and/or brew keg. Fill completely with sanitizing solution and leave for the recommended time (generally 10–15 minutes).

fermenter lacking a tap. As you can see, packaging your beer entails complex choices.

Hygiene is one hazard. The second hazard is to ensure that you have enough carbonation, although not an excessive amount as this could be hazardous, as mentioned earlier. In physical terms, you are looking at a further, secondary, fermentation in a keg or bottle so as to generate an effervescent beer (that is, with enough carbon dioxide to produce bubbles when poured). This secondary fermentation can be generated using residual sugar in the wort, but, as suggested earlier, your beer will be fully fermented with only unfermentable dextrins left. As a result, you are looking to add sugar to the bottles.

This can be done by the spoonful (as shown in Figure 2.30), but a potential hazard is that the granules sink to the bottom and dissolve slowly, producing a layer

Fig. 2.31 Example packaging system showing beer, equipment and working space.

Rinse with clean, boiled water before use, unless using a food-compatible sanitizer.

5. Add the required volume of sugar to each bottle or brew keg using a clean pipette or measuring spoon, ideally sanitized with boiling water.

6. Add the beer into the bottles or brew keg. Pour through a tap with tubing into the bottles, or syphon from the fermenter. Bottle-filling valves are available that can be attached to the tubing. When pressed against the bottle base the valve is released, allowing beer to flow. These make bottle filling very easy as there is less foam generated. However, ensure that they are fully cleaned after use.

To generate a syphon, first fill the tubing with cooled boiled water. Pinch the tubing close to both ends and insert one end into the beer first, then lower the tubing to a jug and release the second pinch. Beer should be drawn from the fermenter into the jug, as in Figure 2.33. Pinch at the jug end of the tube to stop the flow so that you can transfer the tubing to the bottle or brew keg. As you can imagine, this requires some dexterity. Adding a tap to the jug end of the

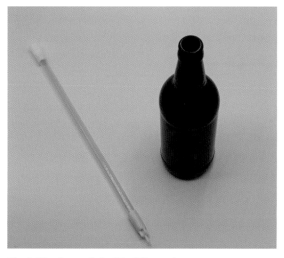

Fig. 2.32 Example bottle-filling valve.

Fig. 2.33   Using tubing and preparing a syphon.

tubing can make the manipulation easier. Delivery valves are also available that release the flow only when pressed and so provide an easier, and less messy, control.

Referring back to the hazards of packaging, you will have addressed the hygiene problem with good sanitation and cleanliness. Similarly, you will have addressed the carbonation by carefully managing the residual sugar in the beer. However, there is still the final hazard of oxidation.

This hazard arises when air (containing oxygen) is introduced into the beer, where it can react to produce stale flavours. Think here of the aroma of soggy cardboard and you have a close example. Naturally you won't be operating in an air-free environment, so it is difficult to exclude incidental oxygen pick-up. Fortunately, as yeast will remain in the beer, small amounts of oxygen are rapidly absorbed as the cells start to ferment, providing a limited chance to cause problems.

To avoid further oxygen uptake, look to minimize any bubbling of air into the beer, such as large-scale frothing – for example, pouring the whole ferment into a new bucket. Also avoid any long-term exposure. One area to be conscious of is the delay between filling a bottle and capping it. Ideally, fill one bottle and cap one bottle before the froth collapses in the neck, rather than filling twenty then capping twenty. Working alone makes rapid capping difficult, but an assistant can make a welcome difference.

Various options are available for capping bottles. A simple double-lever crimper will work but is sometimes difficult to keep stable, so an assistant can be valuable to hold the bottle steady. A pillar capper (*see* Figure 2.34) is ideal. Whatever your choice, ensure that the caps are fully and tightly crimped so that air cannot enter – or beer leak out. Home-brewing suppliers will be able to provide a check gauge, which consists of a flat metal bar with a hole of the right size to slip over a fully crimped cap.

Fig. 2.34 Capping beer bottles.

A final word on packaging. A good beer is dependent on the residual yeast in the beer to conduct the secondary fermentation. Generally, the level of yeast at the end of fermentation is just right for this. However, if you leave your beer in a fermenter for an extended time – think here of three or more weeks – then most of the yeast will have settled out. Check by pouring out a small glass and if very clear consider a careful stir to re-suspend some yeast, though not so much that the beer becomes murky.

AFTER THE BREW – CONDITIONING

Once packaged, maturation is mostly a matter of time while the beer conditions. Under normal circumstances it will take seven to ten days for the yeast to complete the secondary fermentation and produce the fizz to

sparkle your beer. This does depend on temperature, so keep your bottles or brew keg moderately warm, say around 15–20°C if possible. If the surroundings are very cold, you will need to leave it for longer, but test after a week or so to see. Thereafter you are ready to go. Cheers to your first pint.

Fig. 2.35 Enjoying the taste of a first pint.

CHAPTER 3

MOVING ON FROM KITS TO GRAIN BREWING

Welcome to your next steps in brewing. Having achieved a perfect pint from kit brewing, the next step is to look at how to produce beer from its raw materials – in effect, a full-scale mash brew. At this stage, you will need to upgrade your equipment and consider a few additional processes. However, the basic understanding remains, along with a focus on hygiene.

As the name suggests, grain brewing leads you

Grain brewing is where you extend your knowledge of brewing concepts and, most importantly, develop key practical skills. In fact, skills and experience are essential requirements to produce good beer. Knowing brewing terminology, enzymology and biochemistry does not guarantee that you will have a drinkable pint. Doing the right things on your brew day will achieve this, even if you are unsure of the reasons.

away from kits and pre-prepared syrups, towards the increasingly extensive list of cereal grains – the mainstay of serious brewing. Here, you are looking for cereals to provide the sugars for fermentation, as brewers have for over 5,000 years.

The greatest difficulty with cereals is that their sugar is not easily available, but is present as starch, that is, an enormous polymer of many glucose molecules. In the barley plant, starch provides the energy reserves for the seed to germinate after a winter of dormancy during which it remains inert. To achieve this in the barley grain, the starch molecules are tightly packed in endosperm cells and surrounded by protein (*see* Figure 3.1). Notice that most of the grain is the endosperm, and thus starch. Try chewing a barley grain and you will quickly see how tough this mix is – although take care of any delicate teeth, which can break if you bite too hard.

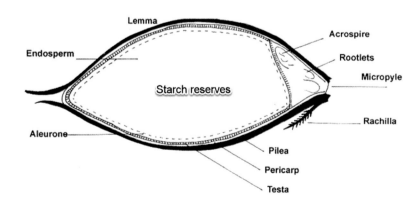

Fig. 3.1 Barley grain showing parts. Note the large endosperm.

In the field in spring the barley grain starts to absorb water and swell. This stimulates the production of enzymes to digest the cells and protein, and exposes the starch to be digested also. The sugars from starch, along with amino acids from proteins, are all funnelled to the embryo, which germinates into a new plant.

As brewers, this is going too far. We are happy to allow the cells and protein to be digested, but don't want to lose the starch as the seedlings use it to grow. Maltsters are skilled in allowing the grains to germinate just far enough to preserve most of the starch and enzymes, then to dry the grains as malt. This is what you use in a mash brew, which will be outlined in this chapter.

BIOCHEMISTRY FUNDAMENTALS

Sugars

Before looking at the process of mashing, it is useful to familiarize the features of sugars, as these are fundamental to the reactions in mashing. Following are the major sugars in brewing, in order of size from smallest to largest: glucose, fructose, sucrose, lactose, maltose, maltotriose, dextrins and starch. Aside from their names, Table 3.1 shows a summary of the features to be aware of.

The sugars encountered in brewing have a common molecular ring structure and are often able to link together to form chains. Starch is an extremely long chain of simple glucose molecules, but is digested in mashing into smaller sugars: glucose, maltose, maltotriose and dextrins of varying sizes, as shown in Figure 3.2. Of these, glucose, maltose and maltotriose are fermentable, while the larger and more complex dextrin sugars are not. Fermentable sugars are converted to ethanol and carbon dioxide and are not found in beer when it is mature. Dextrins, though, are not fermented and remain in the beer and contribute to mouthfeel and body.

Barley provides the source of sugars in the mash, although common table sugar, sucrose or glucose syrups may be added as additional extract.

Table 3.1   The Features of Brewing Sugars

Sugar	Size	Percentage in Standard Wort	Fermentability	Features
Glucose	Single sugar – monosaccharide	Around 12%	High	Very sweet
Fructose	Single sugar – monosaccharide	Very low 2%	High	Very sweet
Sucrose	Double sugar – disaccharide	Very low 1%	High	Very sweet; complex of glucose and fructose
Maltose	Double sugar – disaccharide	High 45%	High	Sweet; complex of two glucose sugars
Lactose	Double sugar – disaccharide	Nil	Nil	Sweet; complex of glucose and galactose; found in milk
Maltotriose	Triplicate sugar – trisaccharide	Around 15%	Moderate	Some sweetness; a complex of three glucose sugars
Dextrins	Sugars of many sizes	20–30%	Nil for most brewing yeasts	Light sweetness; a complex of different numbers of glucose sugars
Starch	Very large polysaccharide	Low	Nil	A polymer or many glucose sugars

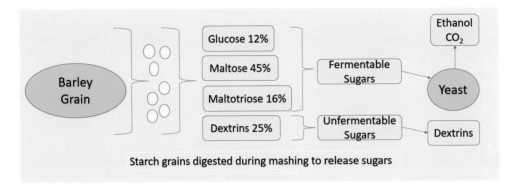

Fig. 3.2 Digestion of barley starch and the range of sugars produced.

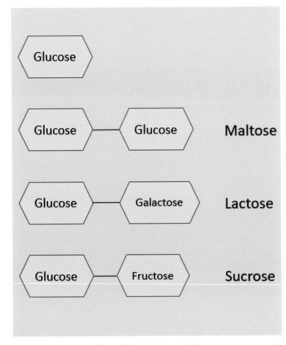

Fig. 3.3 Common brewing sugars, maltose, sucrose and lactose molecules, showing their compositions.

Occasionally, lactose sugar may be added to provide extra sweetness, as it is not fermented by yeast so can be a useful addition to milk stouts. Figure 3.3 shows the structure of glucose, maltose, lactose and sucrose molecules.

WHAT'S HAPPENING IN THE MASH?

In your previous kit brews, a mash brew was used to provide the sugars for fermentation. In a mash brew, these sugars will be generated from the starch in the malt. As mentioned, the enzymes needed to digest the starch (specifically the starch-digesting amylases) are already present in the grains of malt. These and the starch in the grains are dry and in suspended animation until dispersed in the liquor of the mash.

Once the mash commences, the liquor will hydrate the grains and start to dissolve the starch and the enzymes. Being at a warm temperature between 60 and 70°C, this dissolution will occur rapidly and before long the enzymes will begin to digest the starch into simpler sugars (see Figure 3.4). By the end of the mash, you will have a strong mix of simple sugars – glucose, maltose and maltotriose – which can be fermented by the yeast. These sugars are essential to yeast growth and, of course, are converted to ethanol and carbon dioxide. You will also have a proportion of larger sugars, dextrins, which are not fermented, but which will provide body to the beer and contribute to its mouthfeel.

During the mash, proteins will be digested to their component amino acids, which are also essential to yeast growth. Not all proteins will be digested and some will remain in the wort, eventually contributing to mouthfeel and foam. Other nutrients are released from the malt, particularly minerals and vitamins, although minerals will also be provided in the liquor. With standard ingredients and processing, the wort produced from your mash will be a rich mixture of nutrients for yeast to grow. For more details on the dynamics of mashing, see the sidebar 'What Happens in a Mash Tun Bed?'.

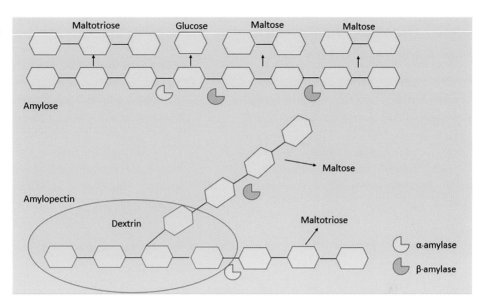

Fig. 3.4 Digestion of starch by amylose enzymes: α-amylase digests all parts of the amylose and amylopectin chains; β-amylase digests bonds at the end of the chains to release maltose. Neither enzyme digests around the branch points, leaving these as dextrins.

WHAT HAPPENS IN A MASH TUN BED?

A mash tun is generally a circular vessel that is insulated to retain heat. It has a false bottom, which is a sturdy plate with holes or slots cut into it. Below the plate is a void leading to the outlet at the bottom.

How you form a mash bed depends on the method of mixing the mash. The first stage is to warm your mash tun using a quantity of hot water. In a commercial brewery, hot liquor is added to the mash tun so that the plates are covered to about 25mm, or 1in. The malt is mixed with hot water at a specific temperature using a mixing device such as a Steel's Masher. As the mash falls, it then entraps air, which will help the malt to float and remain buoyant (see Figure 3.5). The home brewer may add the correct quantity of water for hydration and add the malt carefully to the vessel, mixing to avoid any dry spots. The nature of this mixing will again entrap any air into the grain. In each case, the mash will look like a thick, fluffy porridge.

After the conversion period, the brewer will separate the wort from the mash. The wort is gradually run off and any cloudy wort is returned to the top of the mash tun until it begins to look bright. When this happens, the wort is run to the kettle and the mash is sparged with liquor at 77°C. The key part of doing this is to maintain the mash floating above the plates, so that the liquid run-off is balanced by the added sparge liquor. The run-off balance is to avoid the mash collapsing on the plates and compacting, so blocking the bed run-through. It is the skill of the grain brewer to get this balancing right. A careful, slow sparging at the beginning is also important to avoid channels forming in the mash bed and creating an uneven flow.

Fig. 3.5 A suitable porridge mash consistency.

WHAT DO YOU NEED FOR A MASH BREW?

Scan the pages of a brewing supply catalogue or its online listings and you will find a wide range of equipment to support your mash brewing, from a simple kit to convert a picnic basket into a mash tun, to a semi-automatic computer-controlled vessel. It is therefore advisable to have some guidance to direct your spending. So, what is essential?

The Mash Tun

First, you need a vessel of suitable size – 25ltr for a 20ltr brew, for example, as shown in Figure 3.6. This clearly needs to be robust and not to distort when filled with hot liquor, so it should ideally be stainless steel, although a strong, food-grade plastic will suffice. The vessel requires a tap a few centimetres up from the base and a separation plate above this with perforations to retain the grain particles, while allowing the wort to run through easily. Figure 3.7 shows a typical view of

Fig. 3.6 Your main brewing vessel – example mash tuns with sparge inlet in the lids.

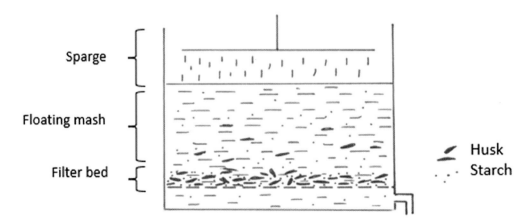

Sparge

Floating mash

Filter bed

Husk
Starch

Fig. 3.7 Mash tun showing internal section.

Fig. 3.8 Your other major vessel – the hot liquor tank.

how the separation plate holds the mash solids behind in the sparging.

The mash tun requires good insulation, as the mash enzymes need a constant temperature to conduct their digestion. A working temperature of between 60 and 70°C will easily lose heat over the hour of a mash, so a double wall with insulation is desirable. If possible, heat losses should be limited such that the mash temperature does not drop more than 1°C. An insulated lid is desirable to limit losses from the top.

The Hot Liquor Tank (HLT)

The Hot Liquor Tank (HLT) is a vessel that will hold your hot liquor ready to add to the mash. It could double up as the kettle (*see* below), but can also be a dedicated

Fig. 3.9a The kettle.

Fig. 3.9b Wort transfer system.

vessel as shown in Figure 3.8. It requires a heat source, generally an electric element, and to be insulated to save heat loss. In some cases, you may transfer hot liquor from the HLT to the mash tun by a jug, but a tap and pipe connection is desirable if possible, in which case it is common to position the HLT above the mash tun – but safely secured.

The Kettle

A third vessel is also needed – the kettle, sometimes known as the boiler or copper from when copper was the easiest material to fabricate. While the HLT can be used as a kettle to boil the wort with the hops, it is preferable to have a dedicated vessel, like that shown in Figure 3.9a. This requires a suitable element for heating, or to allow heating from below on a stove. As with the mash tun and HLT, it is desirable to be insulated so as to reduce heat losses. A loose-fitting lid should give access for hop additions. The kettle also requires a sieve to retain hops and trub at the end of the boil.

The Separation Plate

The separation plate is critical to obtaining a clear wort, as it must hold the solid grain particles as a filter bed. These particles are residues of the malt husk, plus precipitated protein and undigested starch grains. Letting them through the mash plate and into the kettle will produce problems later, as they can be scalded in the boiling and produce a

Fig. 3.11 Section of a compacted grain bed showing entrapment of residual starch and precipitates.

haze in your final beer. A clear wort from your mash tun is a measure of quality and is important to check in the run-off.

To achieve this separation, the perforations in the mash plate need to be a suitable size – between 0.7 and 1 mm in diameter. Some systems have holes, others have slots, and a quality mash plate will have a bevel on the perforations to increase the speed of the flow-through. The separation distance between the perforations should be close enough to allow a rapid run-through, but not so close as to weaken the plates when covered by the mash. Although you are only using a few kilograms of malt, a thin plastic sheet would soon bend and leak particles into the wort. The separation plate should be a short distance above the tap outlet and be supported on flanges or legs to keep stable and allow the wort to drain through. Figure 3.10 shows an example mash plate.

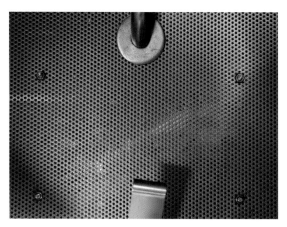

Fig. 3.10 Perforations showing cross section of mash plate and holes/slots.

TAPS AND VALVES

Many types of taps and valves have been developed, but for the home brewer the options are limited. This is because these must be designed with hygiene and safety in mind. When handling hot liquids, stainless steel is imperative for safety.

When choosing a valve, you must consider the valve design itself and how it is connected to the pipework or vessel. Connection can be using a screw-type mechanism with threads such as BSP, RJT or DIN. As you can imagine, the nuts for these threads are not interchangeable. The other connection type is a clamp arrangement with a seal between the parts, such as the Tri Clamp shown in Figure 3.12.

Plastic can be an alternative for the cold side of operations, and these are usually a tapered cock arrangement snugly fitting in a plastic housing. Plastic can be durable, but may suffer from scratches, which could impinge on hygiene. Plastic taps should be designed to be taken apart easily to facilitate cleaning.

Fig. 3.12   Example threads on valves and Tri Clamp.

Professional brewers use a butterfly valve when selecting a closure. It consists of a disc on a spindle, which when turned closes against a rubber seal and stops the flow of liquid. The issue with this type of valve for the home brewer is that the smallest option is $^3/_8$in diameter and quite expensive.

For the home brewer, a ball valve is usually the best option as it is less expensive. It consists of a metal ball on a spindle with a hole drilled through, as can be seen in Figure 3.13. The ball sits in a seal and when the valve is open the hole allows the liquid to flow. Closing the valve, the handle is turned 90 degrees, which presents the face against the flowing liquid.

Hygienic diaphragm valves and taps are available. Here, a rubber seal is forced against the pipe or hole to form the seal.

A good valve is best made of stainless steel, either 304 or 316 grade. The seals in all valves must be made of hygienic rubber – in the case of a ball valve a PTFE cavity seal is ideal. A safety mechanism to prevent accidental opening is needed, especially on a tap connecting a hot brewing vessel. This is usually a collar locking the valve shut, which must be deliberately moved to open the valve.

All valves have their issues, such as wear of the rubber seals. Rubber can become split and harbour bacteria. The seal with the spindles can also hold bacteria. The ball and the butterfly valve can trap particles such as hops. The main issue with valves, and in particular sample valves, is that you must not ignore these when cleaning your equipment. Ensure that your cleaning and sterilizing fluid transgresses these valves as part of a cleaning regime. Always look for the term 'hygienic' when specifying brewing valves, especially post boiling processes.

Fig. 3.13   Example ball valve.

While it is clear that the mash plate acts to hold the mash grains from flowing out with the wort, it is the mash husks and grain residues that do much of the fine filtering. As these build up on the mash plate, they form a convoluted path for the wort to run through with many fine channels. It is these that trap the small particles, particularly the starch and protein, which you wish to leave behind and are embedded in the grain bed (*see* Figure 3.11). As such, the mash bed should be as stable as possible, as any disturbance will allow particles to run through. A solid plate is thus much better than a bag holding the grain, as this is easily distorted. It is also important to ensure that there is a good seal between the plate and the mash tun wall.

Taps and Valves

The tap on your mash tun is more than a handle to turn – it is an important control on the flow of wort out of the mash tun. The internal surfaces of taps are areas where contamination may lurk and require good cleaning directly after use. An easy flow tap on your mash tun will ensure that you transfer the wort rapidly and with limited turbulence. A narrow tap is more likely to clog and be difficult to clear. For more details on the types of taps and valves, *see* the sidebar 'Taps and Valves'.

Sparge Arm

Mashing doesn't stop after 60 minutes of incubation. Once the digestion is complete, it is necessary to rinse the mash while wort drains out for collection. This rinsing is termed sparging and is conducted with liquor of a slightly higher temperature than the mash, generally around 76–77°C, so as to reduce the viscosity of the wort and speed the run-off.

While it would be possible just to pour in fresh liquor, we need the run-off to set up the filter bed of husks and for the rinsing to be as even as possible across the mash. To achieve this, a sparge arm is installed above the mash, either a circle of tubing with regular perforations, or a short length of perforated pipe spinning on a pivot. These perforations are angled to spin the rotation and spray down on the mash. A head pressure of liquor will spray the wort evenly and so rinse the mash thoroughly. Both options can be seen in Figure 3.14.

Either design of sparge system will work, as long as there are enough perforations to cover the surface of the mash. A critical feature, of course, is to ensure that there is enough head pressure and that the

Fig. 3.14   Circular and rotating sparge arm options.

Fig. 3.15a   Hand-held refractometer in use.

perforations are not blocked. Plastic or copper are often used, but stainless steel is preferable if you have the budget.

Refractometer

An important element in achieving your recipe targets is to monitor the gravity of the wort, especially during sparging. Although you can use a saccharometer, this is most easily done with a simple hand-held refractometer, which will give you a result in % Brix – basically the percentage of solids dissolved in the wort. As most of the solids are sugars, the % Brix can be converted into original gravity, then into potential alcohol.

Hand-held refractometers are simple to use, requiring only a couple of drops of liquid on their platform and an observation through the eyepiece. Figures 3.15a&b show a refractometer in use and a view of the scale seen. For more information on refractometer theory and use, *see* the sidebar 'Bending Light to Measure Sugar'.

PREPARING FOR YOUR MASH

Before mashing-in, you need to have a few things ready – as well as a recipe, which will help you to keep track of the steps and remind you what to do and when! The two major components are the grist and the liquor, as these form the body of the mash. You will also need a thermometer, a long spoon, a jug around 1ltr in volume and a timer. If you are looking to adjust your salt balance, you may also need some liquor salts, as these will match the liquor to your recipe and achieve the right pH and flavour balance.

Some basic recipes to trial mashing are outlined in Chapter 9, but many recipes will include more than one type of grain and possibly some adjuncts (non-grain sources of extract). These will all need weighing out and mixing thoroughly in a container. For a 25ltr brew, you are likely to need in the region of 3–6kg of grist.

Although you are looking to brew 25ltr, you will need less liquor than that in the mash tun, as a large proportion of the wort comes from the sparging of the grains after the mash. Nevertheless, more than

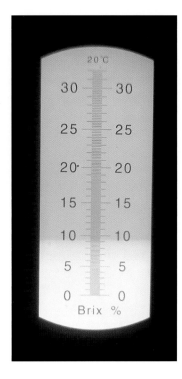

Fig. 3.15b View through eyepiece showing value of 9 on the Brix Scale.

25ltr of hot liquor is required overall, since some will remain in the grains after sparging. If your target mash temperature is between 60 and 70°C, you will need your liquor at a higher temperature, perhaps 80°C, as the grist will be colder and will reduce the overall temperature. It may take a few hours for your liquor to heat up, so advance planning is required.

You will also need more space than when conducting extract brews. For a mash brew, you have more vessels to manage, more manipulations to conduct and also by-products to process. This means more kitchen surface, or a dedicated work area with good access to a sink or drain.

THE MASH PROCESS

Getting your mash right is a fundamental requirement of a good beer. It will provide the right amount of sugar for the yeast to produce the target alcohol. It will also produce the right balance of sugars and other nutrients to support a strong fermentation and will limit the possibility of faults such as stale flavours and hazes developing. In essence, you will be conducting a simple mixture

BENDING LIGHT TO MEASURE SUGAR

Sugar strength can be measured using a saccharometer (a hydrometer calibrated for sugar solutions), or a refractometer. What both are measuring is the amount of sugar dissolved in a volume of liquid. The old definition of a kilogram is the weight of 1ltr of water at 20°C. If you dissolve 40g of sugar in that litre, it will weigh 1.040kg, or 1,040g. Brewers will express this as 1.040°, or just 40°. A hydrometer is a weighted glass or plastic instrument with a calibrated scale on the stem. When placed in a liquid, the hydrometer will float. The density of that liquid can be measured by reading the scale at the surface of the liquid.

A refractometer uses the property that light will bend when it passes from one medium to another. In the refractometer, a prism is used with a higher refractive index than that of the sugar solution, so that a stronger solution bends the light at a greater angle. This angle can be measured on a scale to reveal the density of the sugar in solution.

To use a hand-held refractometer, cool the sugar solution to 20°C. Spread it on the surface of the instrument and close the two halves together. Look through the eyepiece towards a bright light. A dark line will reveal the reading, as shown in Figure 3.17. Most refractometers use the Brix Scale, but this can easily be converted to specific gravity.

One degree Brix is 1g of sucrose in 100g of water, expressed as the actual sugar concentration. Although not strictly true, one degree of Brix is approximately the same as one degree of Plato. To convert Brix to specific gravity, multiply the Brix by four. Therefore 10° Brix will be 1040°. These conversions are good enough for the home brewer, but if you require greater accuracy, tables are available online.

Refractometers are good instruments to use to measure wort strength, but should not be used to measure the gravity during fermentation. The alcohol interferes with the refractometer's readings to give a false result. To measure the gravity of a beer, it is best to use a saccharometer. However, do this on a sample removed from the fermentation rather than leave a saccharometer floating in it, as this may increase contamination.

Fig. 3.16   Saccharometer in use.

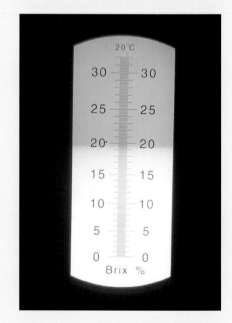

Fig. 3.17   Refractometer scale showing measurement.

Fig. 3.18 Initial collection of wort in jug.

Fig. 3.19 The sparge in action.

of grains and liquor, achieving and maintaining the correct temperature and controlling the collection of wort in preparation for boiling.

Taking the mash process as a series of steps, these are the stages:

1. Warm the mash tun. This is done so that the vessel does not drain heat from the mash. Simply pour in a couple of litres of hot water from a kettle or from your HLT and allow to equilibrate; 5 minutes should do this unless you have a very thick and heavy vessel. When warmed, drain away the liquor.
2. Add fresh hot liquor as the start of the mash. Your recipe will tell you how much is needed, but for 25ltr of a 5%ABV beer this will be around 14ltr.
3. Now start to mix in the grist. Slowly sprinkle on to the liquor and disperse with a paddle or long spoon. You want the grist to be evenly dispersed, so work slowly to produce a smooth mixture without lumps of grist with dry centres. Large lumps will not be digested and so will lose valuable extract and lower the final alcohol level. In contrast, do not over-agitate the mash as this will bring in too much

air, which may oxidize the mash and produce stale flavours.

4. Once well mixed, check the temperature. If on target, leave the mash to incubate. If more than 1°C higher or lower, add small amounts of hot or cold liquor to adjust. If the mash is greatly out of

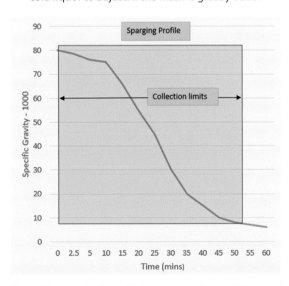

Fig. 3.20 Graph of gravity in a mash and run-off showing window of collection.

Fig. 3.21a   Measuring gravity with a saccharometer.

Fig. 3.21b   Refractometer.

target do not discard it, but instead add enough liquor to bring the mash to between 62 and 70°C. Take a note of the volume added and adjust the sparge volume. You may find that you don't hit your targets for this brew, so check your system for the next mash.

5. Leave the mash to incubate for 60 minutes, during which the reactions to digest the starch will be complete. Do not be tempted to interfere with the mash beyond checking the temperature. Any stirring may produce oxidation and also settle the solids to the bottom where they will be less digestible.

6. After 60 minutes, slowly run off a litre or two of wort from the tap, as in Figure 3.18. Do this progressively and return the wort carefully to the top of the mash. This will start to settle the mash bed to filter the wort as it runs out. Initially the wort will be cloudy as the mash bed is developing, but should run clear before very long. At this point, you can start to collect the wort in the kettle and begin to sparge.

7. Sparge the wort by opening the tap for liquor to run into the sparge system – the sparging ring or arm. You now need to pay careful attention, as the sparge rate should match the run-off rate. If the sparge rate is faster, the mash tun will fill up; if slower, the grains will be exposed and the mash will dry out. This is one of the skills of good mashing practice. Also check the temperature. It should be higher than the mash temperature and ideally around 77°C, so as to decrease viscosity and enhance the run-off. Don't be tempted to go any higher, as very hot water will dissolve astringent flavours from the malt husks, giving your beer a very dry mouthfeel. Figure 3.19 shows a typical sparge in action.

8. As the sparge progresses, the collection volume will increase, but also the concentration of sugars in the wort running out will decrease as they are diluted by the sparge. At what point do you stop collecting? After all, you could rinse through extensively to remove every bit of sugar, but this will dilute the collection and reduce the final alcohol concentration. Your recipe will provide an indication of how much sparge is needed. The best answer to this is to monitor the Brix in the run-off and stop when it reaches around 2% (equivalent to eight units of gravity), as indicated in Figure 3.20. At this point, it is not worth collecting the extra volume of run-through remaining, as it will have undesirable levels of tannins and make your beer astringent.

9. You will now have a collection of wort ready to boil. Once the collection is complete, check the gravity with your refractometer or a saccharometer (using a sample of wort cooled to around 20°C [see Figures 3.21a&b], as the

reading will vary with temperature). If you are following a recipe, you may find that your gravity is lower than expected. However, this is to allow for the evaporation in the boiling, which will concentrate the wort and increase the sugar concentration.

BOILING THE WORT

You now have a kettle of wort to which to add your hops and carry out a boil. Boiling stabilizes the wort by removing excess protein, killing microbes and balancing flavour. Hops are a key element in providing flavour to beer, specifically bitterness and aroma, and are added to the wort as it boils. It is advisable to turn on the heat once all heating surfaces are covered by the wort, so speeding up the boil time. This will also limit the time that the hot wort is in contact with air and so reduce oxidation, as well as minimizing foam.

Recipes often require hops to be added at the start of the boil and at the end. Measure these accurately (*see* Figure 3.22), since hops are quite pungent and small differences may be noticeable.

A typical boil time is 60 minutes. This is ample

Fig. 3.22   Measuring hops with an accurate balance.

WHAT ARE COPPER OR KETTLE FININGS?

Copper or kettle finings are an extract from an edible red seaweed called Irish Moss. Quite often home brewers call it this, but its real name is carrageenan. It consists of long sugar molecules that have a strong negative charge. When added to wort at the end of the boil, it reacts with the positive-charged proteins, causing them to clump together to form large insoluble flocs, which then can be filtered from the wort. These flocs are sometimes called 'breaks' and during the boiling and subsequent cooling process you can see the flocs form. The flocs after boiling are called a hot break; after rapid cooling they are called cold breaks.

By the addition of copper finings, you are removing excess protein, which later in the brewing process can react with tannins or polyphenols to make the beer go hazy. Some manufactured copper finings can have PVPP (polyvinyl poly pyrrolidone) added to the carrageenan, which increases the effectiveness of the mixture as the PVPP reacts with the haze-forming tannins.

Copper finings should be added late into the boil, as the boiling process can decrease their effectiveness. Following the manufacturer's recommendations on addition rates is imperative for a successful result.

Fig. 3.23   A strong rolling boil.

to extract the bitterness from the hops and to precipitate protein. During this time, water will evaporate along with some of the undesirable flavours from the wort, particularly dimethyl sulphide (DMS), which has a cabbage/sweetcorn aroma and is unpleasant in the final beer. Be aware that the steam will permeate your rooms, so keep internal doors closed and windows open if possible. Boiling vigour is a balance between being fierce enough to provide for the chemical reactions, but not so hard that it spills out of the kettle. A rolling boil with a good movement of the wort in the kettle is the target, as shown in Figure 3.23.

Up to 10 per cent of the wort may evaporate during the boil, but if your recipe is well planned this will be accounted for and the final gravity should be on target. If the gravity is higher, it may be reduced by adding some boiled liquor to dilute. If it is too low, a longer boil may be needed – or to accept that you will have a

weaker beer and check the recipe and process for the next brew.

Adding hops is straightforward, but beware not to scald your hands when lifting the kettle lid! The first charge will quickly circulate in the rolling boil, releasing its bitterness and aroma through the boil. The late charge will be added 5–10 minutes before the end of the boil and mostly releases the characteristic hop aromas.

Another late addition to the boil is copper finings, which are often known as Irish Moss. These are typically an extract of seaweed, although some chemical alternatives are available. Copper finings assist in the precipitation of protein to help clarification and require heat to disperse into the beer. Only a small dose is needed, either as a tablet or powder. Check on the packet for the exact quantity needed. For more information on copper finings, *see* the sidebar 'What are Copper or Kettle Finings?'.

At 60 minutes, turn off the heating and allow the hops to settle. A lot of protein and other precipitate will also settle and coat the hops and kettle surfaces in a brown layer. This is termed trub and the boiled wort should be drained from the kettle carefully, leaving both hops and trub behind on the sieve. It should be as clear as possible when it is collected in the fermenter. Collect a jug or two initially and return carefully to allow the trub to concentrate before the wort runs clear.

It is possible to use hop pellets in the boil, but you will need a different system to separate the fine particles of the pellets. For more information on hops, *see* the sidebar 'Hop Cones and Pellets'.

FERMENTING THE WORT

Fermentation of a mash brew is similar in principle to that of an extract brew. The wort needs to cool to around 20°C before you pitch the yeast. During fermentation the wort needs to keep warm between 19 and 23°C if an ale, but cooler, at between 10 and 13°C, for lager.

Unless purchasing a package of materials, a mash brew will require you to inoculate the wort with a suitable level of yeast to ensure a good fermentation.

HOP CONES AND PELLETS

Cone or whole hops are the dried flowers from the hop plant. Hop pellets are made from the flowers by pulverizing them in a hammer mill and extruding the powder through a die to form 6mm pellets.

The purpose of converting whole hops to pellets is to make the hops denser, so easier to store. You can see the difference between the two in Figure 3.24. A further advantage of pellets is that you tend to get more alpha acid or bitterness per kilogram. However, handling each in

Fig. 3.24   Whole hops and hop pellets.

the brewing process is different. The whole hop is typically used as a filter bed, requiring a mesh system to support the hops as the wort is filtered through the hop bed (*see* Figure 3.25). Pellets will not work in this system, as they are too fine to be supported by the mesh.

If using pellets, these are best removed by a whirlpool action. The hopped wort is pumped into a vessel at a tangent to the vessel wall. The centrifugal force ensures

Fig. 3.25   Hops on a kettle filter plate.

that the hops accumulate in the middle when the liquid slows. Try stirring a cup of tea with tea leaves to see the same effect. The clarified wort can then be decanted away. Whole hops cannot be used in a whirlpool, as they will just float. You can, though, use a mixture of pellets and whole hops in a mesh system if you have enough hops to trap the fine hop particles from the pellets (*see* Figures 3.26a&b).

MIDDLE LEFT: **Fig. 3.26a   Whirlpool of hop pellet particles on the kettle sieve …**

BOTTOM LEFT: **Fig. 3.26b   … and in section.**

WHAT IS FOOD-GRADE PLASTIC?

It is important to use a food-grade plastic in your brewing equipment. Additives and some dyes can be leached out of the plastic by acids and alcohol. All plastic containers have an indication of what they contain for recycling purposes. A series of arrows in a triangular image with a number in the middle indicates the type of plastic. Food-grade plastic tends to have the numbers 1, 2, 4 and 5 (*see* Figure 3.27).

- Grade 1 – polyethylene terephthalate (PET or PETE)
- Grade 2 – high-density polyethylene (HDPE)
- Grade 3 – low-density polyethylene (LDPE)
- Grade 4 – polypropylene (PP).

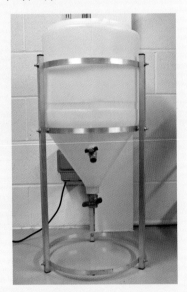

Fig. 3.27 HPPE plastic fermenting vessel.

Polycarbonate, which has food-grade 6, should be best avoided if possible. There are concerns that it may produce bisphenol A (BPA), which is thought to cause health issues, although it is approved for food use. When reusing plastic containers, just be wary of what they contained previously, as any taints may carry through to your beer.

DISPOSING OF SPENT GRAIN, HOPS AND YEAST

What you do with your waste depends on how much is produced and whether you have alternative ways of disposing of it. If you are a commercial brewer in the UK, you have a legal obligation to inform your utility company to

Fig. 3.28a Spent grain and hops …

Fig. 3.28b … from a small brew.

discharge effluent into a drain. You will be charged for the waste and limitations will be set on what you can release. For the home brewer, no such obligation exists.

The quantities of waste produced by the home brewer are small. The typical amount is shown in Figures 3.28a&b and can simply be bagged and disposed of just as you would kitchen waste. Alternatively, if you have a garden it can be composted. Hops were traditionally composted and provide a good nutritional source of nitrogen to plants, although they do take a time to degrade. Hops need to be aerated often in the compost heap and incorporating dry matter such as leaves or sawdust helps the process. Just a word of warning, that hops can be poisonous to cats.

Spent grain can also be composted. As with hops, keep the compost aerated to prevent anaerobic smells. Grain can also be used a mushroom compost and can even be incorporated into some bread recipes. Feeding spent grain to animals is a widespread practice in commercial operations. If the animal is used in the human food chain, then under UK law certain regulations come into force. Feeding to chickens for egg production is certainly an effective way to dispose of waste grain as a useful food source. Small quantities of brewer's grains can be fed to horses – just ensure that the grain is fresh as it deteriorates rapidly, allowing mould to grow and produce toxins.

Waste yeast generated by the brewing process is quite small and often it is simply flushed down the drain to the sewage processing plant. The nutritional value of waste yeast helps to feed the sewage-degrading bacteria. Yeast can also be put on the compost heap, or washed onto the lawn to decompose. The one thing you must not do with yeast is to leave it in a container for any lengthy period. The yeast will decompose, which is called autolysis. The smell produced by autolysis is one of the worst you can imagine and lingers for days!

Fig. 3.29 A valuable use of spent grain – grow your own mushrooms.

Fig. 3.30   Cleaning vessels thoroughly.

during the fermentation so that you know when it is ready for bottling or kegging.

A quick reminder on materials. Stainless steel is the best hygienic material for vessels, but it is expensive so many home brewers use plastic. If you choose plastic, ensure that it is food grade, particularly for fermenters, as your beer will be exposed to it for some time. Further details on food-grade plastics are listed in the side bar 'What is Food-Grade Plastic?

THE CLEAN-UP

Mash brewing leaves considerably more mess and residue than kit brewing, as you will have to remove and dispose of the spent grain in the mash tun and the spent hops left in the kettle. All of your equipment needs a thorough clean and a check for any defects, particularly leaking taps and connections. Mash plates can be difficult to clean, as grains are often held in the perforations and need a thorough brushing (see Figure 3.30). The kettle is likely to have some baked-on hop and trub deposits, particularly on the elements, but be careful not to scour so hard that you scratch the surface. A good soak with detergent can help considerably.

As mentioned for kit brewing, the amount of yeast requires adjusting to the strength of the wort. A standard packet of yeast is suitable to ferment 25ltr of 1.040° wort. For stronger worts, it is advised to add an extra 20–25 per cent for each 10 degrees (2.5% Plato) increase in gravity. Similarly, if your packet of yeast is a few months old, consider adding extra. It is desirable to add more yeast than less, within limits, as a slow fermentation is more difficult to manage and adjust than a rapid one. Remember to monitor gravity

Grain is the larger bulk of your by-products and will rapidly grow mouldy if left exposed. It can be composted, though this may alert insects and vermin, which will be attracted to the tasty sugars and proteins present if left exposed. Figures 3.28a&b shows the amount of grain produced by a typical home brew. A community compost or allotment group would be

Fig. 3.31   Braumeister semi-automatic brewing system.

a good outlet. On a large scale, it can be fed to cattle and chickens and even a couple of kilos would be welcome if you have the opportunity to pass it on. As a last resort, grains and hops can be discarded to your general waste, although alternative uses in baking and growing specialist mushrooms are available, as you can see in Figure 3.29. For more detail on disposing of your by-products, *see* the sidebar 'Disposing of Spent Grain, Hops and Yeast'.

SEMI-AUTOMATIC HOME-BREW SYSTEMS

Different brewing systems have appeared over the years that make home brewing much easier. Especially for those who do not have much space at home, some of these systems consist of one vessel that is both mash tun and kettle, while others are all in one bench-top kits. For those who like to be more hands on, these systems might take away some of the fun, but they can also make life a bit easier and leave less cleaning up to do.

The degree of automatization can vary, with some manufacturers selling pre-prepared recipes where you just add pre-weighed ingredients to different compartments and select the appropriate parameters on the control panel. This is the case for some of the more automated brewing kits, which we could equate to bread-making machines in the baking world.

With these systems, you add the ingredients, then with the control panel or even an App on your phone, you program the brewing parameters, mash temperature and length of boil or hop additions. You can then almost just walk away and leave the machine to it. Some systems include the fermenting vessel and dispensing system, so reducing the space needed and you don't have to buy more equipment. The volumes that these systems produce tends to be around 5ltr, as shown in Figure 3.30.

Other systems can be a bit more hands-on, producing larger volumes – typically 25ltr – and consist of a combined mash tun/kettle, where you add the grist to a basket for the mash. Once the mash has finished, you remove the basket containing the spent grain and proceed to boil in the same vessel.

These brewing systems are particularly useful if you would like to experiment with step mashes, as they can be programmed to increase the mash temperature throughout the process. They generally have a recirculation system, so the temperature will remain constant throughout the mash bed.

These larger systems work a bit differently to those outlined previously. Generally, you would add more liquor to the mash than in a standard mash tun, possibly the full amount of your brew. Sparging, however, would be reduced to compensate for the liquor absorbed by the grain. Aside from being a more compact system, these do reduce considerably the time needed for your brew by reducing the sparge. However, extract efficiency can be affected.

CHAPTER 4

MANAGING MALTS

Congratulations on your progress. By now you will have brewed some extract beers, gained experience with grain brewing and hopefully enjoyed the results of your labours. You will have managed mash temperatures and sparging dynamics, chosen hop additions to a target bitterness and controlled your fermentations to correct attenuations and alcohol levels.

What more remains beyond producing tasteful beers and gaining acclaim from friends and family? Few brewers are content with just the ability to produce a set range of beers. As well as achieving consistency in your beers there are always fresh horizons in sight, new ingredients to try and novel beers to achieve. There is also more knowledge to gain and apply to your brewing.

This chapter focuses in more detail on the features of malts, adjuncts and other extract materials. Your target is not just to know more about malts and the mashing process, but to gain understanding on how

these have been developed to achieve reliable extracts suitably matched to beer flavours and character. This chapter will look in detail at barley varieties and malt production, at their quality assessment and at managing your mash to achieve targets reliably and consistently.

However, it is important to apply this knowledge to practical brewing and to expand experience with different ingredients and processing. As a start, there are a couple of recipes detailed in Table 4.1, incorporating additional concepts in mashing that will be followed in theory considerations. Try them out and test the results using the protocols detailed later.

Recipe 1: Continental Dunkel Beer   Specialist continental malts provide interesting flavours and colours in this rich, malty beer. This recipe substitutes a proportion of pale malt with Munich and Vienna malts to enhance malt character and produce a more grainy

Table 4.1   Trial Recipes to Test Differences Between Grist Mixtures

Ingredient	Recipe 1	Recipe 2	Notes
UK pale malt	85% (4.00kg)	70% (3.25kg)	306L°/kg
Vienna malt	8% (375g)		304L°/kg
Munich malt	2% (100g)		304L°/kg
Wheat malt	5% (225g)	5% (225g)	310L°/kg
Flaked maize		20% (1.0kg)	290L°/kg
Flaked barley		5% (202g)	280L°/kg
Mash liquor	12.7ltr	12.9ltr	2.7:1 liquor to grist ratio

L°/kg (often expressed as LDK) are units of extract from each malt expressed as the degrees of gravity per kg of malt. Check the sidebar on malt features for further details.

and toasty flavour. However, they have lower levels of enzymes than standard pale malt and will require your pale malt to provide these to digest starch to your target extract.

Recipe 2: An Adjunct Mash   This recipe incorporates a high proportion of adjuncts to replace pale malts. Many adjuncts have little colour, so your beer will be lighter than standard beers and have greater opportunity for hops and yeast to show their character. Most adjuncts also have low or limited levels of enzymes, so you will be relying on the pale malt to digest the starch. For this you will need to manage the mash temperature carefully. This is critical to maintain the enzyme activity that will achieve a good extract and your target alcohol. Both recipes are based on a 25ltr brew of 5%ABV beer with mash efficiency of 85%. While you are processing these recipes have a look at some of the details of malts and other extract materials to use in your mash.

WHAT'S MORE TO KNOW?

The general features of barley have already been outlined in Chapters 2 and 3 in the context of starch providing extract for sugar release in the mash and fermentation to alcohol and carbon dioxide. What further detail is useful?

It is useful to have a deeper understanding of the enzyme reactions occurring in the mash and how they affect the extract of sugars and amino acids. By knowing these it is possible to be more assured in controlling mash conditions and interpreting the specifications of different malt varieties. As part of this, it is useful to have a knowledge of biochemistry relating to sugars and of their metabolism to produce flavours.

As well as contributing starch for alcohol production, the mashing process also has important impacts on final beer quality by releasing lipids, which can be oxidized to stale flavours. Another flavour arising from the mash is dimethyl sulphide, also mentioned before, but which requires some control to avoid leaving a vegetable pungency in the brew.

Finally, to note that protein is also a major feature to

MALT FEATURES

L°/kg, or LDK (litre degrees per kilogram), are fundamental units to use when assessing how much extract you can obtain from your malts. The value is based on laboratory tests and is the amount of sugar (or, more strictly, soluble material) that can be extracted from 1kg of malt if mashed into 1ltr of wort. This is, of course, an extrapolation, as it would not be possible to conduct such a thick mash as 1kg in 1ltr. Nevertheless, the standard laboratory test allows the extrapolation and is a critical figure to know when you are calculating your recipe ingredients.

Obviously, the more extractable starch and sugar the higher the LDK value and eventually the more alcohol that can be produced from the recipe. Malts that have been kilned at high temperatures will have lower LDK values, as some of their sugars have been converted to other compounds by the heat. In contrast, some cereals may have higher LDK values than barley malt, as they have less protein and less husk.

manage in mashing, as too much remaining in the wort may result in cloudy beer. In contrast, having too little protein in your beer will make any foam head short-lived, resulting in a flat-looking pint. Balancing protein digestion and retention becomes a difficult target to achieve.

Varieties of barley are a key consideration of all brewers. Malt extract used in most kits will be a mixture of undeclared provenance, but mash brewing allows specific varieties to be selected. As well as differences among barley varieties, there are major differences in the common styles of malt – pale, crystal, amber, brown, black, chocolate and more. Knowing the characteristics of barleys and malts allows beer character to be anticipated and incorporated into brewing recipes. Managing the mash to extract optimal fermentability and wort character is an important brewing skill.

In addition to malts, a vast volume of research has been conducted on using additional sources of extract, partly because they can be cheaper than malt, but also because they are more readily available in different parts of the world, so reducing transport and providing local revenues. Experimentation with some of these is at an early stage, but can be readily applied to small-scale production.

With all of these topics to cover, it is a good idea to start with barley itself, its varieties and selection.

BARLEY: PRODUCTION AND PROCESSING

Travel through the countryside in spring and you are likely to see fields of barley sprouting shoots. By early summer these will be showing ears of seeds or corns bent down on spikelets with a long awn protruding from each corn. Spikelets and awns are a way to distinguish barley from wheat, which has vertical spikelets without awns. By July and August barley corns will have ripened to a golden colour and be ready for harvest. Growing and mature barley plants are shown in Figures 4.1a&b. Wheat is another important brewing cereal but differs from barley, as can be seen in Figure 4.2.

Some barley varieties are sown in autumn to mature early in July, while other varieties are sown in spring to mature later. There is more difference related to yield than brewing quality among these, although many brewing varieties are spring-sown. There are also differences between barleys with six rows of corns and two rows of corns along the stem. Generally, two-row barleys are most commonly used in brewing and have larger corns, with a greater proportion of starch to husk and to protein.

Protein levels are important in specifying brewing barley, as low levels below 12% (also expressed as 1.7% nitrogen) are needed to minimize the amount in wort and beer. A low level of protein reduces issues with haze formation and is an important specification when choosing malt. Cultivating barley for brewing requires careful attention to soil conditions and nitrogen additions. Not all areas have suitable soils and although barley will grow in many climates in the world, not all

Fig. 4.1a Field of maturing barley.

Fig. 4.1b Ripe barley.

Fig. 4.2 Field of maturing wheat. Note the difference in spikelets to barley.

will give good malting results. The UK has a very good climate for producing malting barley and has many varieties available.

As you will probably have seen, harvesting barley is highly mechanized today and is efficiently processed. In past years, harvesting involved teams of workers using scythes and heavy physical labour. This worked well with the tall varieties popular over 100 years ago and which also provided straw for a range of other uses. Mechanical harvesting used today is geared to short varieties, which are also more resistant to being blown over in large fields (lodging). In the move to short varieties, some features of heritage barleys have been lost, but recent initiatives have identified their value and are aiming to reintroduce them through breeding experiments.

Although barley varieties differ in their field yields and in starch and protein content, do the beers they produce differ? Are some varieties better than others and if so, which? This is difficult to determine for sure as malting introduces many other factors, but studies have been conducted that indicate that there are differences in fruit, floral, malty and toffee flavours among the varieties. Other studies using varieties grown in different locations have indicated that malt flavours may also differ according to terroir. Such studies were conducted on pale ales, which lend themselves to detection of subtle flavours. Similar trials using darker beers may not be so distinctive.

How might this apply to a home brew? Once you have perfected and achieved consistency in a recipe, try selecting malt from different barley varieties to see if flavours change. There may, of course, be differences between harvests from different years' weather, so your experiments may require some time to complete. However, this is one area where small-scale analysis may provide interesting information for general brewing.

MAKING MALT: A BRIEF SUMMARY

Dry days are preferred for cereal harvesting, but this can't be guaranteed and barley may be wet when collected, particularly in early mornings. This will encourage mould to grow and attract pests, making it unsuitable for brewing. To avoid this, harvested barley is dried to around 12% moisture and stored while the

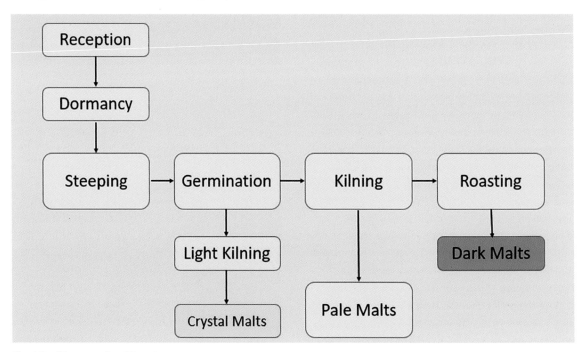

Fig. 4.3   Diagram of malting stages.

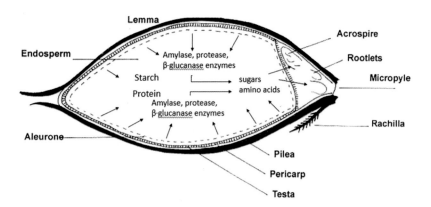

Fig. 4.4 Diagram of enzyme mobilization within the barley grain.

Lemma

Endosperm

Amylase, protease, β-glucanase enzymes

Starch

Protein

sugars

amino acids

Amylase, protease, β-glucanase enzymes

Acrospire

Rootlets

Micropyle

Rachilla

Aleurone

Pilea

Pericarp

Testa

grains undergo their natural dormancy. Dormancy, where the grains prepare for growth, may take weeks or months, during which the grains are carefully monitored to maintain a constant temperature and to minimize deterioration from mould and pest damage.

The malting process is summarized in Figure 4.3. It starts with the grains being steeped (soaked) in large tanks of water to initiate swelling and activate enzyme production. The grains are then germinated in controlled temperatures and humidity to the point of producing some roots and a primitive shoot before they are dried; the shoots and roots are then removed. This germination mobilizes internal enzymes to digest the cell walls and protein that encase the starch grains, so allowing amylase enzymes access to initiate their digestion and release sugars (see Figure 4.4).

Naturally, this occurs on a bulk scale of many tonnes, so requiring extensive engineering to move the large amounts of grain and process it at suitable temperatures to control possible microbial growth. Temperature is a critical feature, as enough heat is required to encourage germination but too much heat will kill the grains. Oxygen is also critical, as too little will encourage undesirable bacteria to grow and produce rancid flavours. A strong air current is drawn through the germinating grains in order to keep the temperature stable, reduce microbial growth and remove carbon dioxide generated by the grains.

Once the grains have germinated to a suitable point – that is, when the starch has been exposed but not digested – they must be dried (kilned). In today's processing this typically occurs in the large germinating

kilning vessels, which can increase the air temperature at a suitable rate to keep enzymes active. Many years ago, the grains would be moved to a separate kiln with a perforated floor and coke would be burnt to dry the grains gradually to a suitable point with enzymes intact. Today, an integrated germinating and kilning system is typically used.

Some malt can be heated further to achieve different degrees of roast to produce crystal, chocolate or black malt with increasing colour. As a reference comparison a light pale ale malt would have a colour rating below 10 EBC (European Brewery Convention) units compared to black malt of up to 1400 EBC units. For more details on malt analysis see the sidebar 'Malt Specifications'.

SO MANY MALTS

By now you will be aware that there is a multitude of malt types – pale, lager, amber, crystal, black, chocolate, Vienna, Munich and so on, all with very different flavours. Heating the grains to different degrees, from a light toasting to a full-scale roasting, is the main cause of this variety. Like coffee, the higher the temperature, the darker and more burnt the grains and the greater the roast flavour. However, in contrast, the higher the temperature, the lower the level of enzymes present in the final grains, as enzymes are rapidly denatured by heat. As a result, dark malts are unable to digest starch and are typically used in small proportions alongside pale malts, which contribute active enzymes for starch and protein digestion.

Roasting is conducted in large rotating drums, as you can see in Figure 4.5, and will produce grains, as in Figure 4.6.

Despite these effects, this is not fully definitive as some malts can be intermediate in colour and enzyme activity. Brown malt, for example, was processed centuries ago by careful kilning to achieve a moderate colour with workable enzyme levels. To do so required workers to work inside the kilns wearing cork boots, certainly not an allowable practice today!

Table 4.3 is a list of the more common malts with their colour levels, extract potential and percentage of nitrogen – an indication of protein content (data from Fawcett & Sons, maltsters, Castleford, UK, but similar to those from other suppliers). Colour is also expressed in other units such as °SRM (Standard Reference Method;

MALT SPECIFICATIONS

A supply of malt should include an analysis to indicate its characteristics. This will allow you to make calculations for your recipes and also to check that it is within acceptable tolerances. The important specifications are those relating to the amount of extract, colour and protein (expressed as nitrogen). Others relate to conformity to safety such as absence of toxins. The table indicates typical specifications for pale ale and lager malt followed by details of interpretation.

A brief warning! It is possible to experiment with malting at home but there is always a risk of mould growth producing toxins, so unless you have a laboratory in which to conduct appropriate tests it is best to rely on commercial malts for your brewing.

Table 4.2 Specifications for Pale Ale and Lager Malt

Specification	Ale Malt	Lager Malt
Moisture (%) maximum	3.5	4.5
Extract on sample LDK	299	296
Extract dry basis LDK	310	310
Colour (°EBC)	5.0–7.0	2.5–3.5
Nitrogen dry basis: total (%)	1.4–1.65	1.55–1.75
Nitrogen soluble (%)	0.61	0.62
Soluble nitrogen ratio (%)	38–43	36–40
Diastatic power (°IoB) Minimum	45	60

How to interpret your malt specification:
- Moisture should be dry enough to discourage mould growth and to keep the grains stable in storage.
- Extract values indicate the degrees of gravity that a kilogram will release when mashed. This is measured in a laboratory-controlled method, but should be indicative for your recipe calculations.
- Colour is the level obtained again when mashed in controlled conditions.
- The nitrogen data are useful to indicate that there will be enough amino acids released to support yeast fermentation. The total nitrogen in the range indicated will show that you won't have excess protein to cause a haze, but enough will be present for yeast nutrition. The soluble nitrogen ratio indicates that the digestion of proteins will be adequate.
- The diastatic power is an indication of the ability of the malt to digest starch and release fermentable sugars.

previously termed Lovibond). To convert SRM colour units to EBC multiply by two.

With so many choices, there is plenty of opportunity to develop a wealth of different beers – as well as modifying standard recipes for common styles. Light and bitter style beers tend to reflect the hops added to provide their character and distinction. Darker beers are more suited to varying the malt additions. Maltsters are increasing their range of darker malts using different kilning and roasting temperatures to generate specific balances of flavour. Look out for these options in ingredient lists. Remember that you only need a few per cent of these in your grist to have an impact.

For light beers look out for pale malts produced from specific barley varieties. In many home-brewing supplies a mix of barley varieties may be used in pale malt, but it is possible to obtain specialist choices. Traditional malting barleys include Maris Otter, Golden Promise and Chevallier (shown in Figure 4.7), but you may be interested in some of the more recently developed malts, which may have specific properties to provide a smoother mouthfeel and less staling potential. For further information on malt specifications and interpreting these for your recipe development, *see* the sidebar on 'Malt Specifications'.

Fig. 4.6 Crystal and black malts.

Fig. 4.7 Heritage barley Chevallier.

Table 4.3   Characteristics of Range of Malts Commonly Available from Suppliers
(data from Fawcett & Sons, Castleford, UK)

Malt	Characteristics	Extract l°/kg	Colour °EBC	Nitrogen %	Application
Pale Malts					
Pale ale malts	Well modified, producing consistent extract within the standard ale colour range, giving sweet and flavourful worts	>306	4–6	1.45–1.65	90–100% of pale ale brews
Lager malt	Light golden colour and sweet wort	>306	4–6	1.45–1.65	90–100% of lager brews
Mild ale malt	Darker wort than pale ale malts	>306	6–7	1.45–1.65	Base for bitters, milds, porters and stouts
Vienna malt	Darker wort, aromatic, sweet, flavourful wort	>304	8–12	1.45–1.65	Lagers and ales up to 20% of grist
Munich malt	Darker wort, aromatic, sweet, flavourful wort	>304	18–24	1.45–1.65	Lagers and ales up to 20% of grist
Wheat malt	Head retention and lacing, dry biscuit flavour	>310	2.5–4.0	<1.9	Wheat beers and adjunct up to 40% of grist
Oat malt	Enhances body, flavour of dark beers	>230	4.0–6.0	<1.9	Adjunct 5–10% of grist
Rye malt	Sweet, biscuity and flavourful	>290	5.0–8.0	<1.75	Adjunct 5–10% of grist
Crystal Malts					
Pale caramalt	Very pale, light, sweet wort	>270	10–15	<1.85	Adjunct 5–10% of grist
Caramalt	Pale, golden colour, very light sweet malt flavour	>270	20–30	<1.85	Adjunct 5–10% of grist
Pale crystal	Golden wort, light, sweet malty flavour	>270	50–70	<1.85	Adjunct 5–10% of grist
Crystal malt	Orange wort, caramel toffee flavour	>270	120–140	<1.85	Adjunct 5–10% of grist
Dark crystal	Adds ruby red colour, burnt toffee flavour	>265	200–240	<1.85	Adjunct 5–10% of grist
Red crystal malt	Dark ruby red colour, strong burnt toffee flavour	>265	300–340	<1.85	Adjunct up to 10% of grist
Crystal wheat malt	Dry, more biscuity flavour than crystal malt	>270	100–150	<1.95	Adjunct up to 10% of grist
Crystal rye malt	Dry, liquorice toffee flavour	>270	100–200	<1.85	Adjunct up to 10% of grist

Malt	Characteristics	Extract l°/kg	Colour °EBC	Nitrogen %	Application
Roasted Malts					
Amber malt	Amber colour, dry, mild coffee flavour	>270	90–100	<1.85	Adjunct for bitters
Brown malt	Darker amber hue, dry, mild coffee flavour	>270	140–160	<1.85	Adjunct for bitters
Pale chocolate	Brown colour, smooth coffee flavour	>270	450–550	<1.85	Adjunct for bitters, milds and stouts, 3–5%
Chocolate malt	Darker brown colour, strong coffee flavour	>270	880–1000	<1.85	Adjunct for bitters, milds and stouts, 3–5%
Black malt	Dark brown colour, strong burnt coffee flavour	>270	1100–1400	<1.85	Adjunct for bitters, milds and stouts, 3–5%
Roasted barley	Dark brown colour, sharp, dry bitter flavour	>265	1100–1400	<1.85	Adjunct for bitters, milds and stouts
Roasted wheat	Softer flavour than roast barley malts	>270	600–1000	<1.95	Adjunct for bitters, milds and stouts, 3–5%
Roasted rye	Dry, biscuity flavour	>260	350–700	<1.85	Adjunct for bitters, milds and stouts, 3–5%
Others					
Peated malt	Phenol: medium 15–25ppm	>308	3.0–5.0	<1.60	Flavour and aroma adjunct
Torrefied wheat	Head retention and lacing in ales	>280	2.5–3.5	<2.10	
Flaked barley	Head retention and lacing in ales	>280	2.5–3.5	<2.10	Adjunct up to 10% in ales
Flaked maize	Flavour reducing, smooth character	>290	2.5–3.5	–	Adjunct up to 10% in lagers

OTHER SOURCES OF EXTRACTS, ADJUNCTS AND SYRUPS

As Table 4.3 shows, barley is not the only cereal that can be malted, nor is it the only source of extract in your mash tun. In fact, you could brew a sort of beer from simple sugars and nutrients, although that would strictly be termed hard seltzer.

Malting is possible with some cereals other than barley. These can produce enzymes to digest the protein around the starch grains and the starch itself into sugars. Wheat, oats and rye are commonly malted and can be used to provide some interesting characters in your beer. Other cereals such as sorghum and millet have difficulties if used in high proportions, as their starch requires a higher temperature to be gelatinized than in standard mashes. The enzymes in these cereals are thus inactivated at standard mash temperatures, so requiring purified enzymes to be added.

Many cereals can be used as adjuncts to provide starch, but few, if any, will provide enzymes. Maize and rice are two common adjuncts used around the world to provide extracts for fermentation. In many cases, they are used alongside standard malts (as adjuncts), but in some they are used on their own with the addition of purified enzymes. These adjuncts are often included in recipes because they are cheaper than malt, but also to dilute the colour of malt worts to achieve a very pale ale or lager. However, if used in high proportions they require incubation in a specialized cereal cooker vessel before addition to the mash. More information on cereal features is provided in the sidebar 'What is Special About Cereals?'.

On a home-brewing scale, a major issue with using adjuncts is to ensure that enough pale malt is present in the recipe so that there are enough enzymes to digest the starch in the mash. Generally, 75% pale malt is required for this, as long as mash conditions are optimized.

Adjuncts also provide their own flavour contributions, as indicated in Table 4.3. These may be extreme in the case of the sweetness from lactose sugar but are typically more subtle, contributing softness or dryness as in wheat and rye, or smooth mouthfeel as from oats. Coffee beans are another

WHAT IS SPECIAL ABOUT CEREALS?

Although many cereals can be used in beer brewing, it is the barley grain that dominates the production. Barley is grown worldwide, the fourth commonly grown cereal seed, and if not suitable for beer manufacture can be used as animal feed.

Barley is ideal for making beer as it is a useful source of carbohydrate, with the seed having about 60% starch. The malting process releases enzymes that break down the starch to fermentable sugars and proteins to amino acids. Barley provides small quantities of vitamins, lipids, oils and other minerals. All of these help as a nutrient source for healthy fermentations. Barley also has husks, which stay on the grain during threshing. This husk protects the seed during malting and allows the wort to filter through during the mash tun process.

Different cereals can be used in beer manufacture, both malted and unmalted. Use of these cereals depends on what is locally available, for flavour dilution or even flavour enhancement, foam stability, reduced gluten levels, or for cost purposes. These cereals can be, amongst others, wheat, maize, rice, oats, rye, millet, or sorghum. If unmalted cereals are used, then malted barley is added to provide starch-degrading enzymes to release the sugars. Wheat cereals enhance foam due to the type of protein present. Maize and rice act as a cheaper source of carbohydrate, but can be used to lighten colour and flavour. They also dilute the haze-forming materials in beer. Oats enhance smoothness, whilst rye can add a reddish hue. Millet and sorghum can be used to reduce gluten content in beers that are suitable for people suffering from Coeliac disease.

Malted barley is the ideal cereal for the home brewer, as it provides virtually everything required for a healthy fermentation, which can lead to a beer having good clarity with a strong head-foaming potential. It also provides that great beer flavour.

Fig. 4.8   Example cereals. Clockwise from left: rye, buckwheat, sorghum and oats.

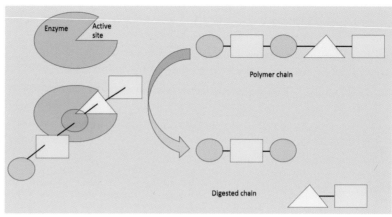

Fig. 4.9 Enzyme active site operating to digest polymer chain.

addition that provide a distinctive character and blend well with those from dark malts.

Another feature that adjuncts contribute to beer is protein, which enhances foam and lacing on glasses. Wheat in particular is often added in small proportions to achieve this and is especially useful if other adjuncts are added to lighten the beer.

Finally, there are possibilities in using simple sugars, particularly table sugar (sucrose), to contribute extract. The simple sugars, glucose, fructose and sucrose, are all readily fermented by brewing yeast and do not need digesting in the mash. In fact, they can be added after the mash directly into the copper. They have a high extract (360L°/kg) compared to malts, so less is needed to produce a set alcohol level. However, high concentrations of sugars do affect yeast metabolism and may encourage the production of undesirable flavours, so use sparingly to avoid a very thin beer.

Granular sugar is, of course, readily available, but brewing sugars may be purchased as syrups (glucose syrup), or as invert sugar, which is sucrose pre-digested to its components of glucose and fructose. Finally, note that honey is a traditional sugar used in beers, historically used to produce braggart but worth considering for a special brew. One important feature of using sugars in the boil is to ensure that they are fully dissolved, as they will settle to the bottom of your boiler if added as a solid block and possibly be scorched onto the element. Careful stirring may be necessary to avoid this.

BIOCHEMISTRY FUNDAMENTALS

Enzymes

As already mentioned, mashing and fermentation depend critically on enzymes, the natural catalysts produced by cells. The activity of enzymes is key to mashing and fermentation, as well as to managing living processes. In the mash they are released from the malt, while in the fermentation they are present within the yeast cells. However, all enzymes have common mechanisms and are affected by similar factors that require careful control.

An important feature of enzymes is that they are proteins made of long chains of different amino acids. These amino acids provide different chemical features to each protein and are in different combinations in each protein. According to their sequence they provide different properties, making each protein unique and with specific chemical abilities. The ability to catalyse and speed up reactions is common to the group of proteins called enzymes and depends critically on their shape. Specific parts of an enzyme have the shape into which other molecules fit, allowing them to be spliced or joined together (*see* Figure 4.9).

Protein chains can be relatively flexible and change shape according to their environment, including the degree of acidity, the presence of salts and, particularly, the temperature of their surroundings. It is for this latter reason that the temperature of the mash and the fermentation must be tightly controlled. Similarly, the amounts of acid and salts in the mash or wort may affect the action of enzymes and how well sugar is extracted, or alcohol produced. If enzymes are exposed to extreme conditions, particularly high temperatures, their shape typically changes irreversibly, so preventing further activity. For this reason, mash temperatures above 70°C have limited success.

Starch and Amylases

Amylase is the term given to enzymes that digest starch into simpler sugars. This is a tough job, as starch is a solid, inert molecule able to resist digestion during barley's dormant period. It is also surrounded by cell walls and layers of protein (*see* Figure 4.10), making it difficult to access in the dry grain. However, when steeped in water during malting, the barley grain is stimulated to release enzymes to digest the cell walls and the protein, exposing the starch grains to amylase enzymes. During germination the starch is progressively digested and the sugars released are used to provide energy for the embryo to grow.

When malt grains are crushed and incubated in a mash tun the enzymes will have direct access to the starch grains. Temperature is critical at this point, as the grains themselves are very solid and will only dissolve if heated. In fact, at a certain temperature they will swell (gelatinize) and open up to allow enzymes easier access. This is one benefit of having a mash strike temperature above that of the incubation temperature.

The effect of enzymes on starch digestion is a combined approach from two major enzymes α- and β-amylase, each of which acts on different parts of the starch. Starch chains are a series of glucose molecules linked together: α-amylase acts on these links at any point except where there are branches; β-amylase acts only at one end of the chain and releases units of two glucose molecules (maltose). Thus α-amylase cuts the chain into different lengths, while β-amylase releases many molecules of maltose – the major fermentation sugar. Together these produce the range of fermentable sugars in wort. They also, by default, produce the unfermentable dextrin sugars that contribute to body and mouthfeel, as neither enzyme can digest the bonds where the starch chain branches.

At this point, the influence of temperature needs further consideration, as α- and β-amylases operate best at different temperatures – α-amylase is more heat-resistant than β-amylase and will be more active at higher mash temperatures (65°C and above), while β-amylase is less heat-resistant and will be more active at lower mash temperatures (below 65°C). In consequence, mash temperatures between 60 and 65°C will give a higher level of fermentable sugars than mash temperatures between 65 and 70°C. Figure 4.11 shows how these temperature profiles overlap. Selection of mash temperature thus has an impact on the final character of your beer and should be taken into account as part of your recipe formulation.

An additional feature to note regarding the response of enzymes to temperature is that all enzymes have a maximum temperature above which their shape changes so much that they no longer operate. This is

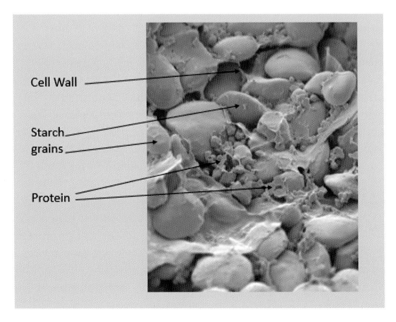

Cell Wall

Starch grains

Protein

Fig. 4.10 Internal contents of barley endosperm showing cell walls, protein and starch grains.

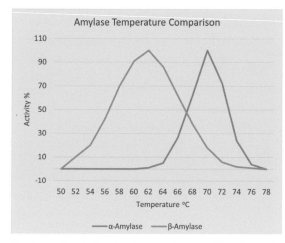

Fig. 4.11 **Graph showing temperature profiles of α- and β-amylases.**

specific for each enzyme and can be as low as 40°C, meaning that they will not function in a standard mash. In contrast, others, such as those from thermotolerant bacteria, can work up to 100°C and have been adapted for industrial use, such as in biological washing powders.

A final question is what happens if the temperature is lower than target? In this case, the enzymes are not harmed, but they will take longer to work. A mash at 50°C, for example, may take up to an additional hour before the starch is digested to target specification.

Proteases

As indicated by their name, proteases digest protein into amino acids – the subunits of proteins. Like amylases, they are synthesized by cereal grains to assist the growth of the embryo. This is partly to remove the protein surrounding starch grains, but also to produce a soup of amino acids

for the growing plant. As yeast also needs amino acids to grow, this has benefits in a mash. One important feature is that proteases work at lower temperatures than standard mash temperatures – generally 50–55°C – and will be denatured and inactive in a typical mash. Many good-quality malts will have their protein digested during malting, but poor-quality malts require a lower-temperature start to the mash in order to digest these proteins before raising the temperature for starch digestion. This is termed temperature-programmed mashing and requires the ability to adjust the mash temperature and a more complex and expensive mash system. The profiles of isothermal (constant temperature) and temperature-programmed mash protocols are shown in Figure 4.12.

REACTIONS IN THE MASH

So, having covered the intricacies of enzyme action, how can the information be used to manage the mash? First, it is important to ensure that your target gravities are achieved by controlling temperature, pH and ion concentrations. Of these, temperature is a physical control, while pH and ions are chemical. Let's start with the physical.

Temperature

Temperature is a measure of heat. The greater the heat input, the higher the temperature, so putting more heat in gets the mash to target temperature faster. However, we also need to consider the intensity of

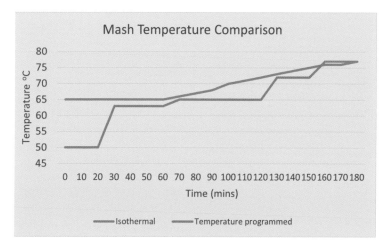

Fig. 4.12 **Temperature profiles of isothermal and temperature-programmed mashes.**

heating processes, as too much heat and a temperature above enzyme thermal limits will cause inactivation. Of course, heat is provided to the mash through the hot liquor, so a heating element is not in direct contact with the grains, thus preventing scorching. Nevertheless, it is possible to inactivate the enzymes if the liquor is too hot – say above 80°C – so control of this is important. Starting your mash with boiling water would certainly result in failure.

The final mash temperature will result from the heat in the hot liquor and its interaction with the lower-temperature malt. To achieve this, the hot liquor will need to be higher than the mash temperature, as the malt will cool it to a considerable extent. As a rough rule, a strike temperature of between 7 and 10°C above target mash temperature will be suitable, depending on the season. Taking temperature readings during the mashing-in will allow you to judge this and add in cold or hotter water if needed. Calculators are available on brewing websites to determine the temperature of your mash liquor depending on target mash temperature and that of the malt before addition. In general, a strike temperature of between 72 and 75°C is a good target but beware of exceeding 85°C.

When testing mash temperature, check in more than one location in the mash tun – side to side and upper and lower depths to be sure that the mix is evenly distributed. Variations between these indicate that the insulation is inadequate or damaged, possibly through impacts or just age causing insulation to compact.

Heat losses are a factor in managing your mash, as you are looking to maintain a constant temperature with no more than 1°C loss over 60 minutes. Losses greater than this can affect the character of the beer through altering enzyme activities. Good insulation is key to keeping temperatures constant and should be built into your mash tun, with a double-skin construction providing space for insulation materials.

Probe thermometers are typical for temperature measurement, but consider purchasing a logging thermometer to record temperatures through the mash and show any variations. An example is shown in Figure 4.13, indicating the rate at which the initial temperature stabilizes and how sparging temperatures change.

Mash Thickness

Mash thickness is another physical feature worth monitoring as will also affect the efficiency of enzyme action. Thicker mashes (around 2.7:1 liquor to grist ratio) will provide more protection of the mash enzymes, particularly α-amylase, allowing them to be more active. Thinner mashes (3:1 liquor to grist and above) will be less protective and reduce mash efficiency. Again, this is a choice you can make in your recipe development and operations, but be aware that diluting the mash during incubation may influence the character of the final beer.

pH

The pH value is a secondary control for your mash efficiency, measuring the level of acidity present and thus a chemical effect. This relates directly to any liquor treatment you have conducted – particularly acid addition to neutralize alkalinity from carbonate salts, but also calcium salts added for flavour. A target mash pH of 5.3 is recommended, as this enhances the activity of the amylase enzymes and ensures a suitable starch digestion. The pH of the mash will directly affect the pH of the final beer and its shelf life. Too high a mash pH and beer pH, say above 4.5, then the greater the potential for spoilage bacteria to grow. Control of mash pH does depend primarily on your liquor treatment to neutralize carbonate alkalinity. Nevertheless, additions

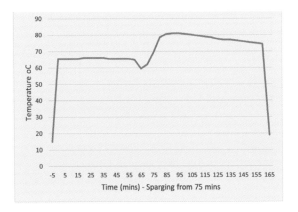

of acid to the mash are possible – for example, if including an acidic fruit extract.

Measuring pH accurately requires a laboratory pH meter, which can be expensive. More affordable hand-held instruments are available and will give an indication of pH. The glass probe is the most sensitive part of the system, so ensure this is not damaged and is cleaned regularly to prevent protein accumulating on the surface and causing inaccuracies.

Mineral Ions

Hydrogen ions are the basis of pH, but many other ions will be present in your mash. Particularly important are calcium and zinc. These are directly involved with enzyme activity, providing essential co-factors. These ions will also be provided from your malt and in your liquor treatment and unless you have an unconventional recipe will be in a suitable range.

MONITORING YOUR MASH

You will have plenty of opportunity to check your mash as it proceeds, although it is recommended to avoid disturbance as much as possible. Introducing oxygen by stirring is likely to lead to increased staling of the wort, while too much stirring may knock the grains to the bottom and stop them floating free.

However, temperature can be monitored continuously with a suitable probe and, as mentioned, if coupled to a logger can be recorded as part of your quality control. Gravity is also relatively easy to measure if using a refractometer, as you only need a few drops for a test. It is more difficult to measure pH, as this ideally requires a pH meter (see above), although some pH papers are more accurate than standard litmus papers, which just show acid or alkali.

Particularly useful is to conduct analyses of the wort production and to calculate the efficiency of your mash. At a basic level this requires a measure of the final gravity of the collected wort and its volume to obtain the litre degrees produced. For example, a collection of 22ltr of a wort with 1.045 specific gravity would have $22 \times 45 = 990$L°/kg in total. This can now be compared to the expected extract of the malts and adjuncts used in the mash. If, in the above example, 4kg

CALCULATING MASH EFFICIENCY

Calculating mash efficiency for each brew is important in helping you to improve and understand your recipe development. Building up a picture of what efficiency you achieve with different strengths of beer or styles will give you the tools to hone your recipe calculations. It will also help to improve your techniques to get that extra pint of beer produced and so save money and time.

Any efficiency is simply a ratio of outputs over inputs. In the example here of calculating mash efficiency, it is all the sugar gained at the end of the process in L° divided by the extract added to the mash in L°.

Measuring the outputs is simple. Take the volume in your fermentation vessel at the beginning of fermentation and multiply it by the degrees of gravity. So, if you produced 20ltr at 40°, this would be 800L°. You could equally measure the volume and gravity in your brew kettle to measure outputs.

Inputs are based on all the materials that have supplied extract or sugar to the recipe. This will include malt, adjuncts and any sugar used. Take, as an example, a beer made using 3.5kg of pale ale malt, which has an extract potential of 300L°/kg; 3.5kg multiplied by 300L°/kg will produce, at 100% efficiency, 1050L°. Therefore, the efficiency of the 20ltr brew noted above is 800L°/1050L°, or 76.2%.

of pale malt with an extract of 305L°/kg^{-1} was used in the recipe, the maximum extract would be 1,220L°/kg and the efficiency would be $990/1220 = 81.1\%$. Another example of efficiency calculation is provided in the sidebar 'Calculating Mash Efficiency'.

A further assessment to conduct with a refractometer is to profile the sparge run-off. This can indicate the effectiveness of your sparging by showing how rapidly the gravity declines. A good profile will show a limited decline initially while the strong worts gradually drain from the grains. This will be followed by a progressive fall as the sparge liquor rinses out the residual sugar, finally declining to an eventual slow finish. The sparge should stop when the gravity reaches 1.008 to avoid collection of tannins and diluting the wort excessively.

A poor run-off would show a rapid fall initially, indicating that the sparge liquor was by-passing the mash grains, possibly through channels produced if the mash bed ran dry, or through any gaps between the mash plate and the mash tun wall. Figure 4.14 shows a comparison of good and undesirable profiles.

The final test of your wort is a tasting. Initially, check for undesirable off flavours such as vegetal, sulphur, phenolic or medicinal. Also look for mouldy aromas, indicating poor storage of malt, and for fetid characters due to bacterial growth. Catching these at an early stage will allow you to reject or adjust your worts and minimize beer problems. For example, too much vegetal aroma is likely to result from certain lightly kilned malts and may be removed by increasing boil intensity. On the other hand, mouldy aromas will indicate that your malt stock is too wet, so encouraging fungal growth. This stock should certainly be discarded, as all other brews will be tainted. Check the advice in Appendix III on ingredient storage.

In a good-quality wort, more positive flavour will dominate. Naturally, wort will be very different to your final beer, but will still have indications of final character. Sweetness will dominate, but look particularly at the aroma, which will indicate the subtle flavours of pale malts and the complexity of the darker malts. With a good malt aroma and taste you will be able to look forward to a satisfying beer and enjoy the efforts of your attention to mash management and control.

EXPERIMENTS TO CONDUCT

Some home brewers aim to produce their favourite beers on a regular basis, consistently and to order. This ensures regular supplies for personal use and to impress friends and family. Other brewers try changes in their processes, to include novel ingredients or combine different malts, hops and yeast, partly for interest in the brewing process and partly to see if a novel beer may arise.

In the latter case, it is relevant to say that brewing is not a fixed science. Although brewing has millennia of history, not everything is known about the processes, or of the beers produced. Scientific studies gradually elucidate details, but often for the benefit of large-scale production. Smaller-scale observations and experiments have relevance to the overall knowledge of brewing and are valid to conduct and report.

If experimentation is of interest to you, here are some areas of study worth considering. As with any experimentation, controls and replication are important, so you may need repeat brews to show consistent effects. Working as a brewing circle may allow this more easily despite differences in equipment and provides encouragement in planning and discussion.

Compare Barley Varieties

Many varieties of barley are developed for agronomical advantage, such as increasing yield, reducing fertilizer and pesticide use, making harvesting easier or, to some extent, enhancing malting efficiency. Effects on flavour are poorly investigated, with few exacting studies.

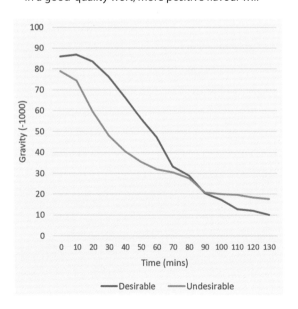

Fig. 4.14   Graph of sparge run-off profile.

Adding Legumes to the Brew

Peas and beans were added to barley and malt in past times when grain was ground at a common mill. The different colours of peas and beans allowed you to know that the crushed grain received back was that which you provided. Legumes contain high levels of easily accessible starch and are good providers of extract to a mash. Experiments have indicated that they have limited effect on beer flavour or character and have an environmental advantage in replacing malt through not requiring nitrogen fertilizers.

Fig. 4.15   Selection of peas and beans.

However, their full effect on different beer recipes is relatively unknown and trial brew results would be a useful indication to the industry. Figure 4.15 shows some example legumes, but many varieties are available to try.

Adding Bread to Your Beer

Like legumes, bread can be a useful supplement to your mash. It contains readily available starch and protein, being derived from wheat. Commercial beer is now produced from unused bread such as loaf ends from sandwich shops, so enhancing recycling credentials. Again, there is limited information on how different types of bread may affect brewing and final beer character. Check out your croissants and toast or other breads, as shown in Figure 4.16.

Try a Parti-Gyle

Before sparging systems were developed, multiple mashes would be conducted on the same grist. Sometimes these would be combined to achieve a wort similar to a sparged mash, but in other cases separate beers would be produced. To achieve this, the wort at the end of the initial mash incubation would be drained out and used to produce a strong ale. The mash tun would be refilled with fresh liquor and remashed to produce a lower-gravity wort for a standard beer. A third mash might also follow to produce a weak table beer. All three worts would be boiled and fermented separately, producing a range of similar beers from one grist.

Try Decoction Mashing

Decoction mashing is a traditional approach to mashing, whereby a portion of the mash is boiled to raise the temperature from an initial 35°C to 65°C in steps. As you can imagine, this increases the brewing time considerably, but some brewers feel that the character of the beer is improved. Check the sidebar 'Decoction Mashing' for further information.

Fig. 4.16   Selection of breads.

DECOCTION MASHING

The decoction mash is a system of raising the temperature of the mash at distinct stages by boiling a proportion of the mash and recombining it together. It was developed in Eastern Europe in a time before thermometers or control systems existed and was used to produce a wort from poorly modified malt. Some brewers persist with the method, as it is said to produce greater depth of malt flavour as well as superior foam potential.

There are three types of decoctions: single, double and triple decoction. Single incorporates a 65°C saccharification stage, whilst double adds a 50°C protein stand. Triple adds a further initial 35°C acidification stage. When heating up the proportion of mash to near to boiling, it is important to do this slowly at 1°C per minute. Decoction mashing is slow and energy-intensive, hence the move to using an isothermal mash conversion system, whereby the whole mash is temperature-raised with gentle stirring by heating systems on the side of the vessel.

CRUSHING YOUR GRAINS

Most cereals used in grain brewing must be milled. This is to open the grain to get better access to the starch and other potential nutrients. This will allow enzymes to work effectively and maximize extraction of sugars and other materials. The purchase of ready-crushed cereals is the easiest way to achieve this. The downside is the extra cost, and the need to store the crushed grain in sealed containers in cool and dry conditions.

The adventurous home brewer may want to mill their own cereals using a hand mill, turning a wheel that can drive two or three rollers to enable the crush. For an extra cost, to save a sore arm, an electrically powered mill can be used. The malt is milled precisely to provide just the right quality for an all-grain brew. An ideal crush will need about 40% husk to enable the free flow of wort through the mash bed. To provide the extract, it will also need 50% grits in even amounts of fine and coarse grits, and 10% flour. Do not forget to have over 75% base malts in your grist to provide the enzymes. Mix coloured malts and cereal adjuncts evenly throughout the mashing process to use the enzymes provided from the base malts.

CHAPTER 5

HOPS AND BOILING

At this point, you have had the opportunity to trial a range of beers with a malt focus and hopefully obtained some useful results and, of course, interesting beers to taste and share. As a next step, you could try some hop-focused beers.

To get started here are two recipes, detailed in Table 5.1, to try with different hop mixtures. Both will emphasize specific hop characters that you can bring out in your beers and use to create distinction, but also to balance with other flavours, particularly those produced by yeast. As before, both recipes are based on a 25ltr brew with mash efficiency of 85%.

This chapter focuses primarily on hops, but also on the boiling process, which has a range of effects beyond extracting bitterness and flavour from hops. Importantly, boiling sterilizes and clarifies the wort, preparing it for the yeast to ferment. Equipment has an impact. Your boiling kettle needs to provide the right conditions for a rolling boil rather than a simple simmer, as turbulence enhances the reactions. The right boiling will give you good-quality wort rapidly and avoid problems later, such as haze and lingering off-flavours.

Table 5.1   Trial Recipes to Compare Two Different Hop Characters
(Full details of processing recipes are available in the Appendix.)

Ingredient	Recipe 1 4.0%ABV	Recipe 2 4.3%ABV	Notes
Malts			
UK pale malt	3.4kg	3.5kg	
Caramalt	600g		
Torrified wheat	200g		
Wheat malt		650g	
Golden naked oats		240g	
Hops			
Magnum	20g		Add to boil
Simcoe	75g		Late addition
Amarillo	75g		Late addition
Challenger		22g	Add to boil
Challenger		65g	Late addition
Cascade		65g	Late addition
Yeast			
American ale	11–25g	11–25g	

WHAT'S MORE TO KNOW ABOUT HOPS?

The general features of hops have already been outlined in Chapters 1 and 2 in the context of their resins and oils providing the compounds for bitterness and aroma and as held in the yellow lupulin glands (*see* Figure 5.1). Both bitterness and hop aroma are very immediate flavours when drinking beers, particularly beers without dark malts. However, bitterness and aroma have different responses in the boil. Bitterness levels increase through the boil, while aroma is progressively evaporated and decreases. In effect, these are contradictory trajectories that

Fig. 5.1   Example hop cones.

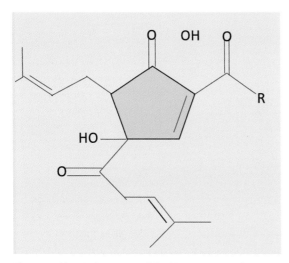

Fig. 5.2   Chemical structure of the bitter compound isohumulone. The R group can be one of three possibilities.

require some skill to manage. Bitterness is one of the most distinctive features of beer. The compound that is responsible for the bitterness taste, iso-α acid, or specifically isohumulone, is shown in Figure 5.2.

Hops and Bitterness

Many plants produce bitter compounds – lettuce and radish are common examples – but they are particularly present in wild, non-cultivated plants. These compounds discourage consumption by animals and so act as protection for the plant. Over time, however, humans have found that in small amounts they add spice flavours to food, making taste last longer and so enhancing enjoyment. Hop bitterness may be considered as an example.

Interestingly, isohumulone is not present in the hop plant, but is produced by heat from humulone, the natural compound in hop resins and often termed alpha acid (α acid). Hops have been associated with medicinal properties for millennia, but were only routinely used in brewing since 1300 or so, when they were recognized to provide protection against bacterial growth and increase shelf life. They were also recognized for providing bitterness and making beer taste last longer.

Hop bitterness has a physiological mechanism. When heated, humulones change their chemical conformation to a shape that fits into human taste receptors and stimulates bitter responses. These bitter compounds are termed isohumulones and are produced progressively through the boil, although the level tends to saturate to a maximum after 30 minutes.

You can calculate the amount of hops needed to achieve a target bitterness using the level of α acids declared by your supplier and an assumption of the efficiency of your boiling. Bitterness is expressed in bitterness units (BU), which are defined as the mg of iso-α acids per litre. Levels range from less than 20BU for light beers up to 60 for strongly bitter IPAs, although some brewers have pushed this to a very bitter limit of over 100 in some brews.

If, though, for example you were to brew 25ltr of a beer with 25BU of bitterness, you would need 25×25 = 625 total mg of α acids. This is, however, assuming a

100% efficiency of conversion to iso-α acids. In small-scale brewing this is never achieved and only 35% may be typical. In the example above, 625/0.35 would be required – 1,786mg or 1.79g. This is the amount of α acids to add, not the amount of hops, as hops are not 100% α acid. In fact, most are less than 10%. If Goldings were to be used with an α-acid content of just 5% the amount to be added is 1.79/0.05 = 35.8g. You can use the above to calculate the hop charge for a recipe by substituting in the equation:

$$\text{Amount of hops (in mg)} = [\text{target BU}] \times [\text{volume}] / [\% \ \alpha \text{ acid in hop variety}] \times [\% \text{ efficiency}].$$

Remember to express the percentage alpha acid and the percentage efficiency as a fraction of 1, where 6% is 0.06 and 35% efficiency is 0.35. Remember also that you can convert milligrams to grams by dividing by 1,000.

Boiling for Bitterness and Hop Aroma

Hops aren't just sources of bitterness, but also of a wealth of distinctive aromas. These arise from the oils in the hops' lupulin glands and vary with hop variety, so allowing for the creation of many different beer characters using hop selection. Nevertheless, certain oils are common and present in many hops and will be expected to appear as you boil the hops in the wort. Interestingly, the various aroma chemicals have different boiling points, so the aroma of your wort will change with time as they evaporate at different rates, allowing you another factor in controlling character. Figure 5.3 shows the chemical structures of some of the most common hop aroma compounds and their boiling points. Figure 5.4 shows a graph of how these will appear in the wort.

It is clear from the time profile that the more volatile compounds – those with the lower boiling points – will evaporate more rapidly than those with higher boiling points. The more volatile compounds will thus be lost faster from the wort as it boils, leaving the less volatile ones behind. The flavours of the more volatile compounds such as myrcene tend to have a more general hop character, while the flavours of the less volatile compounds are more distinctive. Geraniol, for

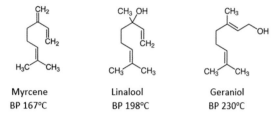

Fig. 5.3   Chemical structure of major hop flavours: myrcene, linalool and geraniol. 'BP' stands for boiling point here.

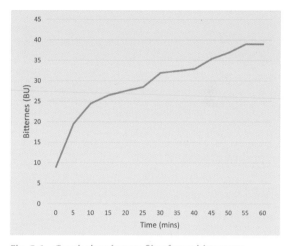

Fig. 5.4   Graph showing profile of wort bitterness development.

example, smells of rose petals or, as the name suggests, geranium. Linalool, in contrast, has a floral, even lavender or orange aroma.

Hop aromas can be grouped into distinct oils with specific flavour associations. Generally, oils are not easy to dissolve in wort and much will evaporate in boiling. Hops with high levels of the more volatile compounds may be best used in late hopping after the boil, or as dry hopping into the beer. The following broad groups of aromatic hop oils are recognized.

Myrcene   Myrcene is present in high levels in many hops and is a flavour easily associated with fresh hops when rubbed. It may be considered as the flavour of green vegetation, but has distinct resinous, piney characteristics. Cascade, Citra and Amarillo hop varieties have high levels.

Humulene Humulenes provide more spicy character with possibly woody and herbal flavours and are more prevalent in traditional, or noble, hop varieties such as Fuggles, Challenger and Goldings.

Caryophyllene This group is common in English hop varieties, providing woody and earthy flavours with some spicy, clove-like character. Again, it is characteristic of traditional English varieties, such as Goldings and Bramling Cross.

Farnesene This oil tends to be present at low concentrations, but shows citrus, herbal and sometimes woody characters.

As a result, you can choose whether to have a beer dominant in any of these flavour fractions, or, potentially a mixture, if you add more hops later in the boil. Such late additions provide an extra charge of flavour and are commonly conducted by commercial brewers to achieve a strong hop punch to a beer. Check in Table 5.2 for a listing of levels of aroma flavours in major hop varieties.

As you can see, hops provide a great opportunity to create distinct and unique beer features. Experimenting with different additions is a great background to gain experience in combinations and additions. Beware, however, as there is always a balance between bitterness and aroma. Some recently developed hop varieties like Citra and Amarillo have high levels of bitterness and aroma, so providing a strong impact to your beer. Mixing hops and their time of addition is an important skill to develop to achieve a target balance in your beer.

HOW AND WHEN TO ADD HOPS

When you develop your recipe, you will need to decide whether to add a single charge at the start of the boil, or to also add secondary charges during the boil, as seen in Figure 5.5. As mentioned earlier, this decision will have an impact on the aroma character of your beer.

Many brewers add an early charge of hops just before the wort is boiling. This exposes the hops to an immediate disruption of their lupulin glands with a rapid release of the α acids and aroma compounds into the wort. Reactions and evaporation start immediately and continue whilst the boil progresses. Some brewers, however, have found that a more interesting hop aroma can develop if the hops are added while the wort is heating up. A gentler release occurs from this, but an understanding of the chemistry is awaited. Perhaps this is an area of experimentation to explore.

Adding hops should be a straightforward process, but beware not to be scalded by steam from the wort,

Table 5.2 Flavour Components in Major Hop Varieties

(Flavour compounds in percentage dry weight)

Hop Variety	Myrcene Floral, citrus, piney	Humulene Spicy, herbal	Caryophyllene Herbal	Farnesene	Total % oil	Total % α acid
Challenger	0.5	0.39	1.25	0.35	2.49	8.5
Fuggles	0.26	0.39	0.13	0.25	1.03	5.5
Kent Golding	0.19	0.36	0.10	0.14	0.79	5.5
Northern Brewer	0.60	0.51	0.18	0.58	1.87	10.0
Cascade	0.55	0.10	0.04	0.29	0.98	7.0
Hallertau	0.14	0.33	0.09	0.45	1.01	5.5
Saaz	0.13	0.23	0.06	0.13	0.55	4.5
Amarillo	1.19	0.23	0.05	0.31	1.78	11.0
Citra	1.71	0.30	0.19	0.45	2.65	13.0

Fig. 5.5   Hop addition to the kettle.

or to let air draughts blow the hops around the room. If your hops are compressed it will help to tease the block apart.

Late additions to enhance aroma impact are typically conducted in the last 5–10 minutes of boil, but some brewers also favour an addition after 30 minutes. Also try letting the wort cool to around 80°C before adding a late charge. Again, experimentation will indicate the effects of these.

To illustrate the effects of different hop additions, try a comparison tasting of the two hop-focused beers from the recipes at the start of the chapter. Beer 1, boiled with Magnum, Simco and Amarillo hops, will show a good fruit character of passion fruit, apricot and some grapefruit. Beer 2, boiled with Cascade and Challenger hops, will have a stronger citrus and floral hop aroma and a light spicy bitterness, clearly different from beer 1. Maintaining the quality of your hops is important to preserve their freshness. Check the sidebar 'Looking After Hops' for further advice.

BOILING

Boiling for Clarity

Hop bitterness will be mostly achieved after 30 minutes of boiling, but it is recommended to keep boiling for 60 minutes. This is to enhance protein precipitation and clarity in your beer. Malt contributes a good dose of protein to the wort, in the region of 1g/ltr. Proteins readily coagulate with heat – as in the

LOOKING AFTER HOPS

Hops are not only expensive, but they spoil very easily. The wonderful aromas soon change to one of cheesy or sweaty socks if left open to the atmosphere. Only buy hops that are vacuum-sealed in metalized foils (*see* Figure 5.6). Make sure the hops are labelled with a date and the alpha acid content. Store these unopened in a cool place. Only buy enough hops to last a brew or two. A year's supply in one packet is not a good idea. If you have an open-packet reseal, thereby removing as much air as possible, you can store the open hops in a freezer. This way they will not lose their potency.

Fig. 5.6   Shrink-wrap hops to maintain quality.

change seen when frying an egg and it turns from clear to solid white. This also occurs in the wort, but with the coagulate appearing as flocs of haze being particularly apparent towards the end of the boil (*see* Figures 5.7a&b for a comparison of these).

Protein coagulates progressively when heated, as the shape of the molecules change and interact with each other and also with polyphenol compounds present in the wort. As the boil progresses, the interactions become more extensive and the coagulation increases in size. The target of a good boil is to achieve a strong coagulation, whereby the flocs are large enough to settle rapidly at the end of the boil and be left behind when the wort is racked into the fermenter.

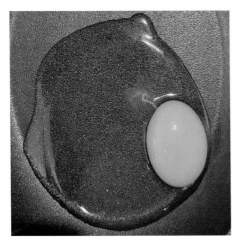

Fig. 5.7a Proteins coagulating in a fried egg.

Factors that enhance flocculation are intensity of heat, time, pH, mineral ions and agitation. A good boil with a strong heating input will achieve a temperature of just over 100°C, which is important. A simmer will be much less effective. The boil should create strong turbulence in the kettle, which assists agitation and the interaction of molecules as they are dispersed in the wort. The pH affects the conformation of protein and will reduce in the boil as acids are

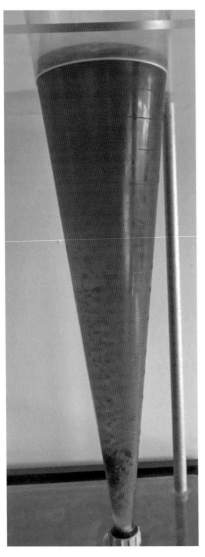

Fig. 5.7b Proteins coagulating in boiled wort.

Fig. 5.8 Trub formation from boiled wort.

released from the hops. Finally, mineral ions can also affect protein conformation, although the standard ions in wort – calcium, sulphate and chloride – are relatively ineffective. Copper, iron and other larger ions will have greater effect, but are not desirable for wort and beer quality. Finally, time is needed for good coagulation, generally 60 minutes, although 100 to 200 years ago a boil of 90 or 120 minutes was practised.

As a test to show the effectiveness of your boil, remove a 100ml sample of wort before the boil and leave to cool and settle in a tall tube or measuring cylinder. Repeat with a sample midway and at the end of the boil. Leave all three and compare the amount of trub at the bottom after a couple of hours of settlement. Figure 5.8 shows the extent of deposit you may get. A good boil should produce an increase in trub deposit showing coagulation.

Boiling for Flavour Balance

Hops are not the only flavour origin in wort. Malt also provides flavour, albeit at lower levels than hops. However, some of these flavours can predominate if not carefully controlled. Dimethyl sulphide, or DMS for short, is a good example, as it produces a pungent vegetal aroma in the wort, similar to cooked cabbage or sprouts. DMS arises from a chemical degradation of S-methylmethionine, an amino acid present in malt (*see* Figure 5.9).

Fortunately, DMS is very volatile with a boiling point of 37°C, resulting in most evaporating during a rousing boil and not lingering into the beer – although you will certainly smell it in your kitchen or brew room. Problems may arise if your boil is interrupted, or the wort simmers and fails to release DMS. In such circumstances, it may accumulate to high levels and become a major flavour in your beer. DMS may also be noticeable if you use certain malts that are lightly kilned, lager malt for example, or if you include unconventional materials in the mash.

A poorly boiled wort may also develop grassy aromas in a similar mechanism to DMS, so ensure that your boil is vigorous for a full 60 minutes and allows steam to escape.

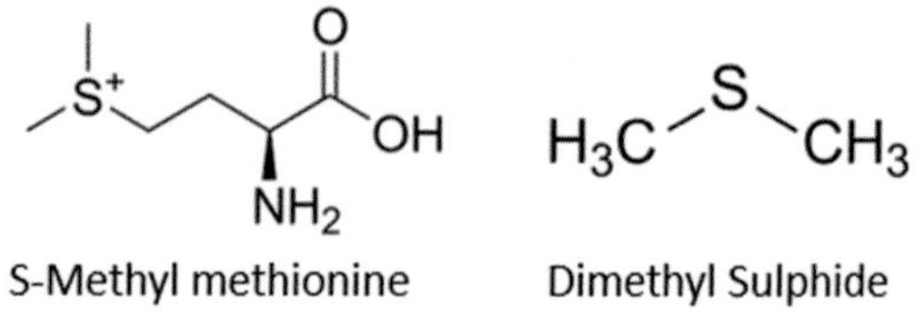

Fig. 5.9 Chemical structure of two major sulphur compounds in wort.

Boiling for Sterility

Another purpose of boiling is to sterilize the wort, so giving the yeast a strong start in fermentation. Absolute sterilization won't be possible at home or even in many commercial conditions, as there is likely to be some exposure of the wort to the atmosphere, allowing potential contamination. However, this will be at a very low level unless the room is very dusty, or your fermenter poorly cleaned.

Despite being incubated at over 60°C during the mash, wort will have a range of residual microbes, which may colonize in fermentation and possibly cause flavour and clarity problems. Some of these are heat-resistant (thermotolerant), or even able to grow during mashing (thermophilic), while others may be spores that will germinate after cooling. Avoiding long mashes, such as overnight, will limit production of undesirable flavours from occasional bacteria and fungi that can tolerate the conditions, as well as a thorough clean after finishing the mash.

A 10-minute boil will kill the vast majority of cells and many spores, while a 60-minute boil will be even more effective. As mentioned previously, good hygiene during transfer to the fermenter is paramount in maintaining the sterility of your wort, so ensure that all surfaces and tubing are well sanitized.

Boiling to Concentrate

Evaporation is an inevitable consequence of boiling wort and a more concentrated wort will naturally result. With an open-top kettle, you may achieve a 10% reduction in wort volume, meaning that the specific gravity increases by 10%. This can be a useful way of raising the final alcohol concentration and achieving

Fig. 5.10   Evaporation by vigorous boiling.

a stronger beer, as you would be limited to about a 1.080 gravity from mashing alone. If your aim is a strong beer above 1.080 gravity, it may be preferable to increase gravity by evaporation rather than by adding simple sugars, which may alter the metabolism of the brewing yeast and introduce undesirable flavours.

Of course, evaporation takes energy – in fact, much more energy than just heating a liquid, so you will find that your brew costs more in power if you evaporate 10% of the wort than if you evaporate just 4%. Keeping the kettle lid partly open will reduce the overall evaporation. Nevertheless, you do need to release some steam, as it will carry away the undesirable flavours such as DMS and so purify the flavour balance. In this sense, it is desirable to avoid extensive condensation of steam back into the brew.

LATE AND DRY HOPPING

Hops may be added to the beer directly after boiling, or later in maturation. In commercial breweries additions directly after the boil are typically conducted in a hop back vessel separately from the kettle, but it is equally effective to add hops into the kettle once the boil has finished. This is also true for high-aroma beers as a heavy a dose of hops may be added at the end as well as at the start of the boil. Some bitterness will be added, but the major effect is to supplement the aroma punch with volatile flavours.

While direct addition to the wort is effective, a greater extract can be obtained by using a pressurized system. This enhances the release of flavours and has become an interesting addition to wort processing. Often termed a hop rocket or hop gun, a pressure system fits between the kettle and chiller, allowing wort to flow through a tight packing of hops that provide additional filtration of protein and thus a clearer wort. Figure 5.11 shows an example hop rocket.

Dry hopping is a different concept, with different results to the standard addition of hops to hot wort. In dry hopping, the addition is to the fermented beer. The aromas released differ and provide yet another dimension of flavour. Certain varieties of hop such as Citra, Cascade, Simco and Hallertau, are particularly suited to dry hopping, but all varieties will provide some character. In general, geraniol and linalool are predominantly extracted, along with polyphenols, which increase mouthfeel. Limited α acids are removed, so bitterness does not increase noticeably and may even reduce, as iso-α acids may be adsorbed to the hops. Hops may also release enzymes, which can result in digestion of dextrins and other changes termed hop creep.

One limitation of dry hopping is the time taken for

Fig. 5.11   A hop rocket.

the aromas to be released, which can be up to ten days for full effect. This suits commercial production, where it may take a week for a cask to be delivered and served in a bar, but it means that you need to plan ahead if your beer is required for a particular function.

EFFECTS OF FERMENTATION

The character of beer once boiling finishes is not immutable. Considerable changes are likely to occur during fermentation and maturation. In fact, the contribution of yeast flavours is extensive, as will be outlined in Chapter 6. However, fermentation also affects some of the flavours produced in the boil. In some cases, this is due to their evaporation in the stream of carbon dioxide produced by fermentation. In others, it is due to enzyme action on the flavours themselves. Geraniol is an example as it may be converted enzymatically to citronellol, which not only has a lime-like flavour itself, but also acts synergistically with geraniol to enhance citrus flavours. The enzymes for this conversion of geraniol are carried by yeast and at particularly high levels by non-brewing yeast such as *Brettanomyces*. Accidental contamination or deliberate inoculation of the wort with such yeasts may have an impact on specific flavours.

SOME EXPERIMENTS

What developments are brewers interested in to modify their boiling and hop contributions? Here are some projects that may be of interest to try at home.

Use Home-Grown Hops

Home growing is increasingly popular and easy to manage, as hops will grow in many climates. Care is needed to ensure that the cones ripen well and to harvest before autumn weather causes wind damage, but many varieties can be productive. As measuring α-acid levels is difficult, home-grown hops may be best suited to contributing aroma, but experimentation may give you a guide to bitterness potential. *See* the sidebars on 'Grow Your Own Hops' and 'Green Hop Beers' for more information on using your own hops. An example of what you can grow at home is shown in Fig 5.12.

Fig. 5.12   Home-grown hops.

GROW YOUR OWN HOPS

Hops are common to the UK and are often found in hedgerows throughout the land, but are commercially grown in Kent, Herefordshire and Worcestershire. The reason for this is not simply because of microclimate. Before mechanization, hops were traditionally gathered by the working-class populations of the east ends of London and Birmingham, who used the opportunity for a paid working holiday, away from the urban sprawl, in their nearby countryside.

Growing hops can be both rewarding and frustrating. They are vigorous growers, but are somewhat susceptible to pests and diseases. You can buy bare root plants from November – just look online for suppliers. For less than £10 you can purchase your favourite variety of hop. Hops are sent as rootstocks wrapped in moss, as shown in Figure 5.13. On receipt, keep moist until planted.

Prepare the ground using as much compost as you can as they can be 'hungry' plants. Plant the dormant rootstock into the ground when hard frosts are past, in a sunny position and keep well-watered. Prepare a structure for the bines, as they can grow quite tall. If you do not have the height in your growing area, they can be trained, with time and effort, to grow horizontally. When the plant is established, select the three or four strongest shoots and keep the base of the plant clear to inhibit pests. Feed the plant regularly throughout the growing season (see Figures 5.14a&b).

Early September will produce your hop cones, and pick them when ripened. The cones will be full of the yellow lupulin when

Fig. 5.13   Fresh hop supply ready for planting.

GREEN HOP BEERS

Although common now, the original green hop brew was invented by Trevor Holmes in 1992, when he was head brewer at Wadworth and Co. in Devizes. This beer was called Malt & Hops. That harvest's recently dried hops and green hops were collected from the farm on the day of brewing, as green hops simply do not keep! The dried Early Bird Goldings are added to the copper at boil with a rate of 1.66g/ltr. From the concept in the 1990s, dried hops have always been used simply due to the sheer bulk of the wet hops. The same rate by experience was used, as the α-acid content was not known at such an early stage of harvest.

they are ready (*see* Figure 5.15). Dry the cones naturally by blowing air over them gently. When dry, store by sealing them in a plastic bag, removing as much air as possible and ideally freezing until ready to use. A hop bine also makes an attractive decoration. The hop plant can be cut back and mulched to protect the rootstock during winter. The plant, if well-tended, will grow back year after year.

Fig. 5.14b   Hop plants in full leaf.

Fig. 5.14a   Hop plants at early growth.

Fig. 5.15   Home-grown hop bines with cones ready for harvest.

Fresh green hops, again Early Bird Goldings, are added in two stages. A proportion of hops is added 15 minutes from the end of the boil, whilst the rest is added to the hop back (hop tea) prior to wort addition. The rate of addition is in the order of 3.5g/ltr, which looks an exceptionally large figure, but takes into account the 80% moisture content of the green hop.

The very nature of not knowing the yield of resins from that season's hops always leads to an unpredictable brew each year and a variable degree of bitterness. The flavour from the green hops is quite resinous, like retsina wine, and is unique. This is the one beer where you get the true vintage of the hop harvest – the 'Beaujolais Nouveau' of the beer world.

Compare Different Recipes

Hop aroma is perceived differently according to your beer ingredients, resulting in different impressions even if using the same hops. Test this with light pale ale and dark porter recipes, but with identical hop additions. Many interactions occur between hop aroma compounds and other components in beer, particularly myrcene, which accounts for up to 75% of total hop oil.

Pre-Boil the Hops

Some brewers are adding hops into the wort before the boil starts and finding that different flavour profiles emerge due to a slower increase in heat exposure and the effect on volatile kinetics. A more extreme approach is to boil hops in fresh liquor separately from the brew and mix into the wort. Boiling myrcene in water is known to produce perillene, a compound with strong citrus/lemony notes that will have an impact on your flavour balance.

Add Other Botanics

Hops aren't the only herb you can use to flavour your beer. Historic beers were flavoured with many other botanical infusions, often termed gruit. Bog myrtle, yarrow, juniper and caraway are examples and can provide interesting alternatives or additions to your standard brew. Beware that some historical additions such as wormwood can be toxic in high doses and be sure to identify any wild collections carefully. The sidebar 'Gruit' has further information.

GRUIT

Before the use of hops, gruit was the term used for the ingredient mixture added to wort or beer to flavour and help preserve the ale. The common herb used to flavour beer was bog myrtle, or sweet gale. Other herbs and spices were also used, such as yarrow, rosemary, ginger, caraway, cinnamon and junipers, amongst many. Gruit herbs may be added to beer directly into the boil or even to the fermenter, but records show that they were often blended into a potage, which was infused for some time before addition. This is an area of potential historical research for brewing students.

In Britain, the term ales indicated that the drink was flavoured by a gruit mixture. After the introduction of hops, beer became used to describe the hopped drink. This distinction between ales and beers has now been lost and the two terms are interchangeable. The variation and availability of herbs for gruit would have led to many different flavour combinations and provide interesting possibilities for investigations today.

CHAPTER 6

YEAST AND FERMENTATION

This chapter outlines the detailed features of fermentation and, inevitably, has a focus on yeast, which is responsible for the process. It also provides information on what is happening in your wort as it ferments and what, and how, flavours develop. Importantly, it provides guidance on managing your fermentation and how to interpret, and correct, problems. For the brewer, fermentation is a quiet time compared to the activities of the brew day. The wort is collected into the fermenter and pitched with yeast. You can now leave it to ferment and produce beer from the mash that you so carefully managed.

This is not to say that the ferment should be ignored. An occasional monitoring is desirable to ensure that the reactions of fermentation are proceeding to plan and that the wort sugars are being converted to alcohol. Sampling and testing will allow these checks to be made directly on the beer, as well as providing an opportunity for a tasting. Today, non-intrusive monitoring is available to allow tests to be viewed from your phone, so limiting the potential of contamination.

A typical fermentation will be complete within five to seven days, depending on the strength of the beer and the fermentation temperature, after which the beer can be chilled to mature before packaging.

YEAST

An essential element of fermentation is the activity of yeast, so a good understanding of yeast physiology and metabolism helps in the control of your ferment and the character of the final beer. Here are some of the features to check.

What are Yeasts?

A simple answer is that yeast is a form of fungus. As such, it has similarities to mushrooms, but is a microscopic, single-cell version compared to the filaments that make up larger fungi. As with most fungi, yeasts can produce spores – although these are not found in brewing yeast. A unique feature of yeast is that it reproduces by budding rather than by dividing in half like bacteria. In budding, a new cell develops directly from a mother cell, gradually grows and then separates, as shown in Figure 6.1.

A key to the understanding of yeasts is to view them in the general taxonomy of microorganisms and particularly their position as fungi. Taken in order of size, the full range of microorganisms extends from viruses through bacteria into fungi, protozoa and algae. For brewing considerations bacteria and fungi are the major groups of concern and although viruses do infect cereal crops and hops, these are of

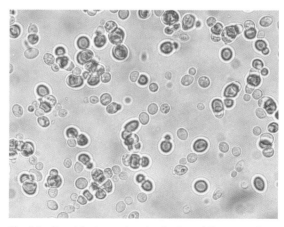

Fig. 6.1   Yeast features showing buds and the general shape of brewing yeast.

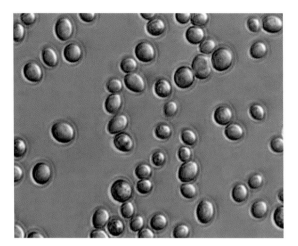

Fig. 6.2a Microscopic appearance of a brewing yeast strain.

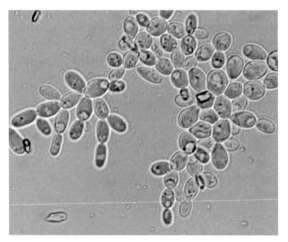

Fig. 6.2b Microscopic appearance of a different brewing yeast strain.

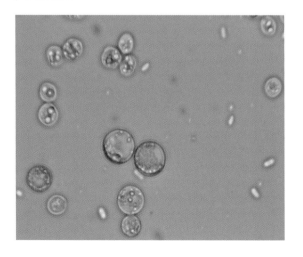

more direct relevance to growers, maltsters and hop merchants.

Looking at brewing yeast cells in the light of a microscope gives a good view of their features – generally oval, budding when actively reproducing, and with some internal components, often a vacuole and granules. Each strain will have its own appearance, which will be distinctive when compared under similar conditions, so it is good to recognize this for the yeast you are using. Shape is the most distinctive feature, with variations seen in the size of mature cells, in their dimensions and internal arrangements. The examples in Figures 6.2a&b give a view of some different strains showing clear differences, while Figure 6.3 shows brewing yeast in poor condition with large internal vacuoles.

What Types of Yeast are Available for Brewing?

Nearly 4,000 species and strains of yeast are listed in the UK National Collection of Yeast Cultures (NCYC), of which 1,400 are ale yeasts (*Saccharomyces cerevisiae*) and 60 are lager yeast (*Saccharomyces pastorianus*). Other collections have equally large numbers. The *Saccharomyces* genus comprises eight species, all of which are active sugar fermenters. A strain of yeast is a variety of a species with distinctive characteristics and abilities. This range gives a wide variety available for brewing different beers and it is interesting that many listed by the NCYC are historical and may not have been used for some time.

The ale yeast is believed to have been present for millions of years and since its first use in brewing has been selected for its abilities to produce good beer. For example, genetic analysis indicates that genes responsible for certain flavours in some ale strains have mutated and these strains were then selected for commercial brewing. *Saccharomyces* yeasts used in brewing other types of beers retain these genes and show distinctly different flavours – wheat beers for example.

Fig. 6.3 Aged brewing yeast showing enlarged size and granular contents.

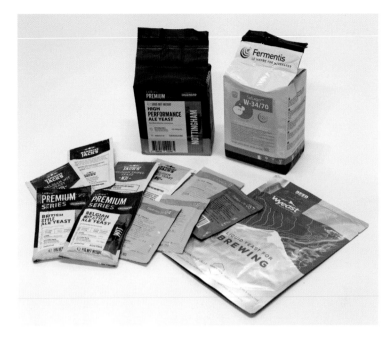

Fig. 6.4   Packets of brewing yeast.

An increasing number of yeast strains is now available for home brewing, each with distinctive properties, cultured in controlled conditions to ensure purity and packaged for long-term storage. Many of these are spray- or freeze-dried powders, while others are live yeast in suspended animation. Advances in understanding yeast physiology have allowed these yeasts to be fortified with nutrients and primed to start fermentation rapidly. The sidebar on 'Powdered Yeast' provides further background, while some example brands are shown in Figure 6.4.

Other sources are available, particularly live yeast from a commercial brewery. This is certainly worth exploring, as it will provide a distinctive character as well as saving on costs. Be aware, however, that live yeast cropped from a brew will have a short shelf life of around seven days before it starts to die off. It must be kept at refrigeration temperature – although not frozen – to maintain its viability. If kept for longer, it will be necessary to pitch more to compensate for the increased dead cells. However, dead cells will give the beer a harsh, yeasty bite or meaty aroma, so beware of using very old yeast. Growing a starter culture is a useful way to ensure that your pitching yeast is fresh. Check the sidebar on 'Growing Yeast Starter Cultures' for details.

POWDERED YEAST

Most yeast suppliers provide their yeast in the powdered form of spray- or freeze-dried granules. These have a good shelf life of many months in the packet and are easy to use with a direct addition to your wort or, in some cases, reconstitution in warm water.

Not all yeasts dry successfully, as the process puts the cells under stress, which reduces viability, but manufacturers are increasingly able to fortify cells and the range is continually expanding. It is also possible to supplement cells with nutrients so speeding their fermentation, particularly if used in high-gravity worts. An increase in yeast numbers is also needed to ferment strong worts – generally add 20–25% extra for each 10° degrees of increased gravity above 1.040.

Dried yeast granules rapidly absorb water and oxygen from the air, both of which activate metabolism and lead to the cells using up valuable energy reserves. If not pitched into wort, these cells will become exhausted and either fail to ferment well or die. Once opened, use the packet and do not rely on a part-used batch from a previous brew. Finally, do not be tempted to freeze yeast. Unless cryopreserved, the cells will expand as ice crystals form and burst.

GROWING YEAST STARTER CULTURES

If you are keen to broaden your brewing microbiology, consider cultivating a starter culture before your brew. This will bulk up yeast numbers and give a greater chance that fermentation will take successfully, as the yeast will already be active rather than recovering from a dried state.

For a starter culture you will need some sterile wort and clean conditions for inoculation. A sanitized 2ltr PET mineral water bottle will suffice if emptied and handled with care. Gently boiling 1ltr of fresh 1.040–1.050 wort for 15 minutes should give a suitable sterility, but keep it covered whilst cooling and transfer to the bottle with care. Pitch with a good inoculum of your yeast (ideally 10–20 million cells per ml or a light to moderate turbidity) and incubate at a warm temperature for 48 hours before pitching.

It is critically important to ensure that the bottle top is left loose during fermentation to allow carbon dioxide to escape and prevent the bottle exploding. Using glass bottles is not recommended for this reason. Chilling when complete will settle the yeast and allow the supernatant to be discarded before use and reduce transfer of any undesirable flavours to your brew.

What Does Yeast Contribute?

Yeast's contribution to brewing is clearly the ability to ferment sugars into ethanol and carbon dioxide, as well as producing a range of other flavours, particularly fruity esters. Ethanol, of course, is at the heart of beer and will be produced in proportion to the amount of sugar present in the wort.

Carbon dioxide is also a major feature and levels in beer must be managed within target levels – generally between 2 and 7g/ltr. This provides the sparkle in beer and although a low level of 2g/ltr will not effervesce

Fig. 6.5   A lively, well-carbonated beer.

with bubbles, it will still be perceived as lively on the tongue. A beer with lower levels will be flat and lacking character generally. Figure 6.5 shows a beer with bubbles forming and supporting a solid head. More CO_2 is produced than is needed for a good carbonation and while the surplus evaporates it is important to retain enough to provide the target level.

BIOCHEMISTRY FUNDAMENTALS

Metabolism

To explain the fermentation process fully it is useful to refer to a metabolic chart (see Figure 6.6). Here the process is shown progressing from the wort sugars into intermediate compounds of pyruvic acid and acetaldehyde before the ethanol is produced.

The wort sugars, glucose, maltose and maltotriose, are taken into the yeast cell progressively, with the simplest, glucose, first, followed by maltose and finally maltotriose. Maltose is digested into two molecules of glucose and maltotriose into three molecules of glucose. Enzymes catalyse these digestions and the

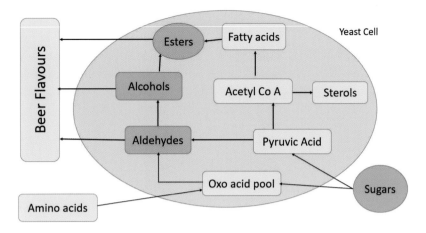

Fig. 6.6 Metabolic chart of fermentation and flavour production.

different reactions in the production of ethanol and are inherent in yeast cells.

Because enzymes are very temperature sensitive it is important to keep your beer fermentation within limits. Too low a temperature and the reactions will take too long or simply stop; too high and the enzymes will be denatured and also stop working. Target temperatures of 19–23°C for ales and 10–13°C for lagers are advised, as these produce the best flavour profiles. Yeast will work and ferment at higher temperatures, up to 45°C in some cases, but the flavour balance at these temperatures would be very undesirable.

The intermediate compounds of fermentation can impact on your beer's flavour profile, for example acetaldehyde, which has a green apple aroma. It is the further reactions of these compounds that have more impact, however. Alcohols react with acids to produce esters, many of which have strong fruit

flavours – banana, peach, apricot and so on, as noted in Table 6.1. These are attractive in many beers, so may be encouraged by your selection of yeast strain and management of fermentation.

Stressful conditions are associated with high ester production. Low pitching rates, for example, will stress yeast and cause increased ester levels, as would very high pitching rates. Similarly, low levels of oxygen at pitch, plus low temperatures or low nutrients as with high adjunct levels, will also increase ester production.

WHAT HAPPENS IN FERMENTATION?

Aside from yeast producing ethanol and carbon dioxide, other changes occur in fermentation and provide an indication that your brew is progressing satisfactorily. Two important changes that you will see are the appearance of a foam and the clouding of the beer due to the increase in yeast cells.

Foam on the top of your beer is a good sign that the yeast is active and also allows you to judge how well the fermentation is progressing. Initially, within 24 hours, a very loose head will appear with large bubbles (see Figure 6.7). Sometimes called a cauliflower head, this will contain many dead cells from the pitching, along with precipitated trub. Ideally, skim off and discard this trub as it may cause a hazy beer later.

Table 6.1 Flavours Associated with Esters Produced by Fermentation

Ester	Flavour
Ethyl acetate	Nail-polish remover
Isoamyl acetate	Banana
Ethyl hexanoate	Red apples
Ethyl caprylate	Apples, pears, anise
Ethyl butanoate	Pineapple
Octyl ethanoate	Orange
Pentyl butanoate	Apricot

Fig. 6.7 Early fermentation head.

Fig. 6.8 Mature yeast head.

Subsequently, a thicker head will form, composed of a dense layer of yeast cells and more protein trub. This yeast tends to be the best quality for reuse and can be skimmed and stored. The cells in this will have had limited exposure to alcohol and be more viable. Figure 6.8 shows an example of this. Finally, a tighter head may form with a high level of dead cells, but which provides a suitable barrier to contamination and so should be left until the beer is mature.

In recent years conical fermenters have become popular. These allow easier yeast management, as the cells settle into the base cone where they can be easily drawn off through a tap directly into a container or into your next brew. The beer in a conical fermenter will not show the same head formation as in an open fermenter, but the sediment will have the most viable yeast in the centre of the cone. Conical fermenters are also easier to monitor and are often supplied with a temperature-control system and good insulation. A

Fig. 6.9 Example conical fermenter.

Wi-Fi link showing gravity fall is a great way to keep track of a fermentation and may include a control to initiate chilling when it is complete.

Your fermentation will also show an increase in turbidity as it progresses due to the increase in yeast numbers. This will decrease, however, towards the end of fermentation because yeast cells typically flocculate together to produce flocs that settle rapidly to leave clearer beer. Flavour changes may easily be detected in fermentation as sugars and sweetness decline but fruity esters increase. This change may allow bitterness to be more apparent, while carbon dioxide will provide the sparkle of carbonation. Your wort has now become beer, albeit green, immature beer.

HOW CAN FERMENTATION BE MANAGED?

Getting a strong start to a fermentation is key to success. A suitable concentration of healthy yeast should get the fermentation going within 12 hours, with a strong head crop and output of carbon dioxide. A view of the head formation should appear, as in Figure 6.7. Maintaining the target fermentation temperature is key, as cold conditions and low temperatures easily lead to yeast stagnating and fermentation stopping. Even if you collect the wort to the fermenter at a temperature above 20°C, it will rapidly cool if your fermenter lacks insulation or heating.

If you are reusing yeast from a previous brew, ensure that it has been kept in good condition and is not too old. A maximum recommended storage of seven days in fridge conditions is advised, ideally undisturbed and without any additions that may stimulate growth and fermentation.

Fermentation control has some quite specific targets, particularly around achieving the final gravity or attenuation. Managing this requires some application of the biochemistry noted earlier. Here, the main difficulty is to ensure that the yeast can ferment the maltotriose sugars at the end of fermentation. Glucose and maltose will be used first, to form the bulk of the ethanol production. Fermenting maltotriose, however, requires more effort and may not occur if yeast is in poor condition, or lacking enough nutrients at the start of fermentation.

Oxygen is often key here and is needed to assist the cells to synthesize their cell membranes. A deficiency in the wort at yeast pitch may lead to problems when the yeast has completed a number of buddings. A lack of nutrients such as zinc and vitamins may cause similar results, so it makes good practice to ensure that your wort is from a full malt mash and not diluted with other extract sources. If you have used high levels of adjuncts, particularly sugar, it may be necessary to add nutrient supplements or yeast food. *See* the sidebar on 'Yeast Supplements' for more information.

YEAST SUPPLEMENTS

Often referred to as yeast food or yeast aid, supplements can be a valuable addition to your fermentation, particularly if your wort has had a low level of malt in the mash. Supplements typically provide nitrogen compounds and mineral ions, particularly zinc, which may be deficient in such worts, but which may also stimulate some yeasts in standard worts.

However, be aware that too high a level of mineral ions, particularly zinc and magnesium, can be inhibitory or even toxic and so slow the fermentation. Follow instructions as to dose rates, and monitor fermentation to determine their effectiveness. In addition, keep supplements dry and away from contamination sources, as they will readily encourage growth of bacteria, yeasts and mould.

The profile of your fermentation should look like that in Figure 6.10, whereby the specific gravity takes a day or so to start falling, but then declines rapidly to target attenuation over the next three to four days.

While the specific gravity falls, the acidity increases. This can be monitored by the pH, which will decrease ideally from a mash pH of around 5.3–4.0 in the final beer. As noted previously, this will depend on your

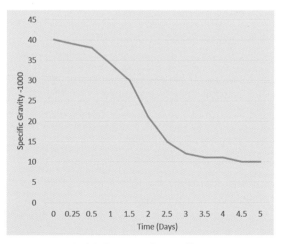

Fig. 6.10   A suitable fermentation profile.

liquor treatment, but in general be aware that a final beer pH above 4.5 may have a short shelf life and be more liable for microbial spoilage.

A further feature to monitor during fermentation is the clarity of the beer. This will decrease initially as yeast multiplies and clouds the wort, but will decrease as yeast flocculates and settles once the beer reaches its attenuation point. Taking a sample will give an indication of this, but viewing in the microscope will provide an indication that this is happening to the yeast cells – as well as showing their condition.

BASIC MICROBIOLOGY

It is not essential to know microbiology to produce good beer – but it helps. In particular it assists in avoiding or managing contamination problems. Here is a summary of the essential features and concepts to be aware of when managing your fermentation.

Yeast and Bacteria

Bacteria-like cells are believed to be the first-evolved microorganisms. They are small in size (around 1 micron in diameter, which is about a tenth the size of a yeast cell). Their cell structure and contents are relatively basic, consisting of an internal cytoplasm containing enzymes, a strand of DNA and ribosomes to synthesize protein. In some circumstances, storage materials may also be present. A cell membrane surrounds the cytoplasm, preventing the contents leaking away but also controlling the entry of materials, particularly sugars and amino acids. Externally, they have a cell wall that is relatively complex, containing many structures to help the cell stick to surfaces, recognize materials, or to move. The cell wall also provides shape to the cell whilst being flexible enough to grow.

Yeast cells are more complex than bacteria, with specialized internal organelles including a nucleus containing chromosomes of DNA, mitochondria for energy, vesicles and vacuoles containing solutions and, like bacteria, enzymes and ribosomes in the cytoplasm. They also have a cell membrane and cell wall that act to recognize and control materials moving into and out of the cell, keep the cell shape intact and provide protection.

Brewing yeast is necessary for fermentation, but non-brewing or wild

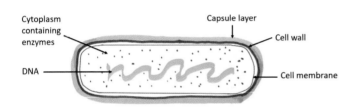

Fig. 6.11a   Diagram of bacteria.

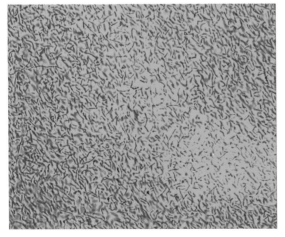

Figs. 6.11b   Images of bacteria.

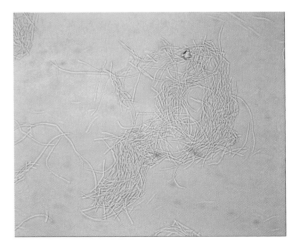

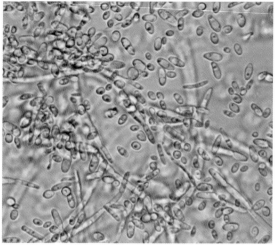
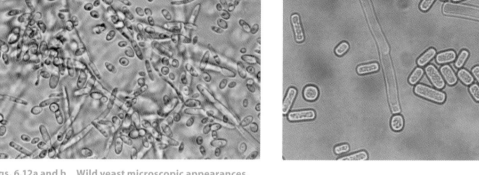

Figs. 6.12a and b   Wild yeast microscopic appearances.

yeast can cause problems and result in spoilt beer. Wild yeasts are often different in appearance to brewing yeast, as shown in Figure 6.12.

Wild yeasts are ubiquitous in the atmosphere, particularly as inert spores. As there are so many species, they can cause a wide range of problems, but often are apparent by producing spicy or medicinal flavours. They are less likely to flocculate, so resulting in hazy beer. More information on wild yeast is available in the sidebar 'Wild Yeast'.

Microbial Growth

Both bacteria and yeast multiply by producing new cells identical to their parents. Bacteria divide into two new cells of the same size, while yeast buds a new cell that eventually separates and grows to the same size

as the parent cell. Bacteria growth is faster than yeast growth and can easily outcompete yeast in numbers of cells, so it is important to limit their numbers in your worts and beers. Alcohol, acid and hop bitterness all limit bacterial growth, making beer a relatively safe beverage from food spoilage microorganisms. Nevertheless, a few bacteria have evolved tolerance to these and can grow in beer, causing spoilage.

The two most common contaminant groups are the lactic-acid bacteria and the acetic-acid bacteria. These produce their respective acids, so spoiling beer by making it sour. In addition, they contribute other undesirable flavours and cause hazes. There is an interesting and fundamental difference between these two groups of bacteria in regard to their need for oxygen. Acetic-acid bacteria will only grow if

Table 6.2   Control of Contamination from Different Sources

Source of Contamination	How to Limit
Air	Avoid exposing beer to dusty environments. Limit steam and high humidity. Keep doors closed when beer is exposed, for example at packaging.
Surfaces	Swab surfaces before and after brewing. Limit dust in the air.
Hands	Wash before brewing and between operations, for example between malt handling and yeast preparation.
Insects	Minimize waste food and general dirt. Keep doors shut.

oxygen is present (aerobic growth), while lactic-acid bacteria grow more actively without oxygen (anaerobic growth).

As a result, lactic-acid contaminations are more dangerous for your beer as once they are present, they will grow readily. Acetic-acid bacteria only grow when beer is exposed to air and thus not during fermentation. Instead, you are likely to encounter them in dispense or if your keg has a leak. Good hygiene will limit the presence of these in the brewery, but it is impossible to eliminate microbes completely, as they will be present in the air, on surfaces and on ourselves. Some useful advice on reducing potential contaminations is listed in Table 6.2.

WILD YEAST

Not all yeasts are suitable for brewing. The standard fermentation species *Saccharomyces cerevisiae* certainly is and for many years was regarded as the primary choice for brewing ales. *Saccharomyces pastorianus* is now recognized as a separate species adapted to lager brewing, having in the past been considered a strain of the ale yeast and variously titled *Saccharomyces uvarum* or *Saccharomyces cerevisiae* var *uvarum*.

Over 1,000 strains of the ale yeast, *S. cerevisiae*, are recognized, with differences in their genetics, physiology and brewing potential, and are increasingly available to home brewers. Many other species of yeast exist, however, and are commonly found in the environment and, in a few cases, as clinical pathogens. Such wild yeasts are, in some cases, generally termed non-brewing yeast, but in fact many of them will ferment, albeit with variable results.

Commercial brewers are increasingly interested in identifying species and strains of non-*S. cerevisiae* yeast, which can provide novel characteristics to beers. In some cases, the beers produced may be considered as sours due to the production of acid, but in others interesting flavour profiles may result, providing opportunity for new beers to be created.

The identification of such wild yeasts as substitutes or partners of standard brewing yeast is exciting, as novel yeast may provide very distinctive flavours, perhaps elevated in esters or phenolics. In other cases, however, undesirable flavours may appear. There is plenty of opportunity to experiment, with the prospect of creating very different beers, or of enhancing fermentation processes such as speed of fermentation, attenuation or clarification.

Two areas of more specific interest that are relevant here are the ability of wild yeasts to produce beers requiring amended fermentations and to produce potential health benefits. In the former case, low-alcohol beers can be produced using yeasts such as *Saccharomycodes ludwigii* and *Zygosaccharomyces rouxii*, which will only ferment glucose and not maltose or maltotriose. Only a limited level of alcohol will be produced and with careful management can be kept below regulatory levels – typically 0.5%ABV. Work is still progressing with such applications, as different yeast species are likely to produce unconventional flavours and require careful testing to avoid any undesirable flavours.

Another specific application is the identification of yeasts that have health benefits, such as probiotic potential or production of nutrients. In fact, it is well known that yeast produces high levels of vitamins during fermentation, particularly the B vitamin group. As a result, yeast tablets have been sold as a health aid for many years. Today, there is increasing interest in probiotic microorganisms, with lactic-acid bacteria and bifidobacteria strongly promoted in health markets. Yeast may also be probiotic by inhibiting the growth or action of bacteria pathogens, although only one yeast, *Saccharomyces bayanus*, is recognized officially. The use of this in brewing is still being evaluated, but it has been identified in historical yeast samples.

SOME EXPERIMENTS

Yeasts offer considerable opportunities to experiment with your home brew and to investigate very novel fermentations. Fermentation microbiology is a very active area of research, with new species and strains regularly being developed for commercial use. Many of these strains are available from suppliers, but it is also possible to isolate yeast yourself from fermented foods and even the environment – although caution is advised on using environmentally sourced yeasts, as pathogens may be included. Here are some options to try.

Commercial Comparisons

Separate a batch of wort into four or five demijohns and pitch each with a different commercial yeast. Try ale, lager, wheat beer, Belgium and Saison for an initial comparison, but many others are worth testing. Ferment at the same temperature and plot their gravity profiles, final attenuation, clarity and final flavour.

Mixed Yeast Cultures

Traditional brewing until the 1970s, and in a few breweries today, typically involved mixed strains of yeast that had evolved over time to provide a cooperative fermentation. Specific strains may have had different abilities, but the overall collaborative growth would have given a broader range of flavours and potentially greater ability to ferment different ingredients. It is inevitably difficult to judge which strains would be suitable to mix, but if you have conducted a comparison of commercial strains, then you may have useful data to suggest combinations – for example, a yeast that attenuates well with one producing a desirable flavour. *See* the sidebar on 'Mixed Strains of Brewing Yeast' for more background.

Repitch the Yeast

Reusing yeast has been the traditional practice for hundreds of years, but it has become a neglected art in the days of readily available commercial dried yeasts. Repitching does require judgement in order to select and crop the yeast at a suitable time, generally between 30 and 40 hours of fermentation. Expect your

MIXED STRAINS OF BREWING YEAST

For centuries beer was brewed with a mixture of yeast strains, but today many commercial beers use a single strain with a balance of abilities. Mixed strains can provide interesting variations in fermentation and in your final beer. However, they can be difficult to manage, particularly when one strain becomes dominant and also when it is difficult to tell strains apart. Figure 6.13 shows an example of two clearly different strains. Mixing pure strains is an option and not just between two brewing strains, but between a brewing and a wine or cider strain.

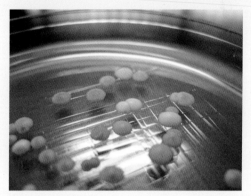

Fig. 6.13   Mixed yeast strains growing on agar media.

crop to be twice as much as needed for another brew, so giving you plenty to share or as a reserve. Cropped yeast will keep in good condition for seven days if refrigerated (but not frozen), so use within this time.

Ferment at Different Temperatures

Temperature greatly affects yeast metabolism and can be interesting to vary for different yeasts. Cooler temperatures tend to produce more limited flavour levels, while higher temperatures will produce more flavour generally, and fruity esters in particular. For example, try fermenting ale yeasts around 25°C and lagers towards 20°C. Not all results will be positive, but you may find some interesting effects.

CHAPTER 7

BREWING TO A THEME

By now you will have developed both skills and experience to produce successfully a variety of beers using different ingredients and brewing processes. As a practised brewer, you will have tested these and will appreciate your own preferences, as well as brewing for the tastes of colleagues, friends and acquaintances. At this stage, many home brewers develop specialities in their brewing, an opportunity that professional brewers can find difficult as they are brewing for commercial sales. Developing skills in a speciality is where you can gain recognition and appreciation, but also overcome technical challenges and demonstrate your skills at a high level.

This chapter looks at some of these speciality areas of brewing or themes. Some of these involve translating existing practices for small-scale production, but in others you will need to develop novel methods, source unique ingredients, or delve into historical sources. These are the essentials of a progressive and competent brewer and can provide a great sense of achievement. Here are some of those specialist areas and examples of their challenges.

BREWING TO STYLES

You will have already brewed several different styles and perhaps experimented with varying the ingredients of a standard recipe and the brewing process. In many brews these will produce an acceptable and drinkable beer, but, in some cases, they may be at the edge of the style characteristics.

At this point it is relevant to ask certain questions. What is a beer style? Who defines styles? And how have styles developed? This is particularly pertinent when beers are viewed in a broad and international context. The understanding of stout, for example, is very different in the UK than in most parts of Africa, where a strong Guinness is heavily promoted, as can be seen in Figure 7.1. Traditional UK IPA beers are a pole apart from American West Coast IPA brands.

For many years beers were identified in very broad style definitions – beer and ale, bitter and mild, lager and Pilsner. Little definition was available to drinkers and many beers were promoted as brewery brands – Bass, Courage, Whitbread – or sold in generic bottles branded by the brewery, as in Figure 7.2.

The appearance of a more dedicated beer public from the 1970s onward directed attention to specific styles of beer and definitions began to be drafted for

Fig. 7.1   Different packaging of Guinness beers.

competition entries and judges. Three initiators of these were the UK Campaign for Real Ale (CAMRA), the UK Society of Independent Brewers (SIBA) and the American Brewers Association (BA). Today, the most extensive international definition of beer styles is that of the BA, which details over ninety-five different styles. Many of these are regional or country variations on basic styles, such as India Pale Ales or Pilsner lagers, but novel beers are increasingly included, such as smoke beer, coffee beer or field beer.

Each style listed by the BA is defined in terms of perceived appearance, colour, malt and hop flavours, fermentation parameters and body, as shown in Figure 7.3 for English-style India Pale Ale. Chemical characteristics provide more specific and measurable parameters and include original and final gravity, colour, bitterness and alcohol by weight (ABW)/volume. Additional notes allow further details, such as mineral composition and hop sources, to be included.

The UK CAMRA and SIBA definitions are less detailed, covering thirty-four specific styles in twelve general categories. All of these style definitions provide guidance for selectors and judges in beer

Fig. 7.2   Victorian bottles showing embossed branding.

English Style India Pale Ale

- **Colour**: Gold to copper
- **Clarity**: Chill haze is acceptable at low temperatures.
- **Perceived Malt Aroma & Flavour**: Medium malt flavour should be present
- Perceived Hop Aroma & Flavour: Hop aroma and flavour is medium to high, and often flowery. Hops from a variety of origins may be used to contribute to a high hopping rate. Earthy and herbal English-variety hop character should be perceived but may result from the skilful use of hops of other origin.
- **Perceived Bitterness**: Medium to high.
- **Fermentation Characteristics**: Fruity-ester flavours are moderate to very high. Traditional interpretations are characterized by medium to medium-high alcohol content. The use of water with high mineral content results in a crisp, dry beer with a subtle and balanced character of sulphur compounds. Diacetyl can be absent or may be perceived at very low levels.
- **Body**: Medium.
- **Additional Notes**: Non-English hops may be used for bitterness or for approximating traditional English hop character. The use of water with high mineral content may result in a crisp, dry beer rathe than a malt-accentuated version.

Original Gravity (°Plato) 1.046-1.064 (11.4-15.7 °Plato). **Apparent Extract/Final Gravity** (°Plato) 1.012-1.018 (3.1-4.6 °Plato). **Alcohol by Weight (Volume)** 3.6%-5.6% (4.5%-7.1%). **Bitterness (IBU)** 35-63. **Colour SRM (EBC)** 6014 (12-28 EBC).

Fig. 7.3   Example of Brewers Association style definition.

competitions to ensure that entries are judged against similar beers. They also test brewers in providing the specifications for their brewing skills and the boundaries within which brewers can demonstrate their ability to produce interesting variations, suitable balance of flavour and distinction compared to other beers of the style. In some cases, a novel beer can provide the initiation of a new sub-style, or even a new style altogether.

For commercial brewers, style guidelines also provide information to customers on the character of a beer, so assisting marketing. Consumers can use style guidelines to focus any complaints that the beer is out of expectation – a lager that tastes like a brown ale, for example. That said, crossover styles do confuse this – Black IPA, for example.

Styles are not isolated from each other and history shows that each major style evolved with or from other styles according to ingredient and technical developments, consumer preferences or marketing initiatives. The connections and overlaps of styles are an interesting study and demonstrate the factors that are most influential in discriminating styles. An analysis of over 1,500 microbrewery beers indicated that styles tended to group into certain patterns – for example, the darker beers, stouts and porters showed very similar characteristics. However, some unexpected relationships were found, such as golden bitters with mild ales, as shown in the groupings in Figure 7.4.

A comparison in the same analysis, conducted on commercial beers from microbreweries between 2006 and 2018, showed that many styles have become lighter in colour by around 18% and stronger in bitterness by on average 5%. This indicates that styles do change over time and doubtless evolve their character.

Of course, drinkers' preferences vary and change with time and are often influenced today by age and by marketing and food trends. These changes may be reflected in home brewers' preferences where commercial pressures are not a factor. A feature of commercial brewing is to provide a range of beers to cover a broad spread of customer preferences and so enhance overall sales. As such, most breweries produce a portfolio of beers, albeit with a predominance of pale ales and lagers.

If you wish to demonstrate your brewing skills across a number of styles, developing a portfolio of different beers is a good target. This will certainly satisfy a range of your associates and provide a pleasing profile of beers in your cellar or bar. It will also allow you to enter competitions with specified style groups and in some cases compete for the prize of best beer range. A high achievement.

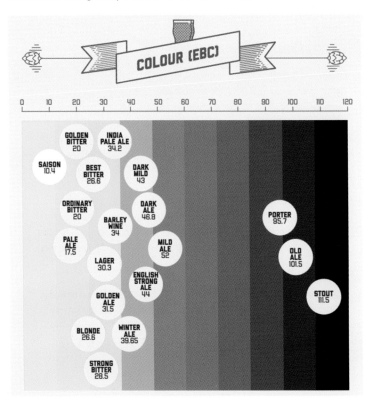

Fig. 7.4   Relationships between UK beer styles in 2018.

COLOUR (EBC)

0   10   20   30   40   50   60   70   80   90   100   110   120

GOLDEN BITTER 20

INDIA PALE ALE 34.2

SAISON 10.4

BEST BITTER 26.6

DARK MILD 43

ORDINARY BITTER 20

DARK ALE 46.8

BARLEY WINE 34

PORTER 95.7

PALE ALE 17.5

MILD ALE 52

LAGER 30.3

OLD ALE 101.5

ENGLISH STRONG ALE 44

GOLDEN ALE 31.5

STOUT 111.5

BLONDE 26.6

WINTER ALE 39.65

STRONG BITTER 28.5

A final question on styles is to consider how essential they are anyway. Many beers are promoted and sold as brands, with limited detail on their contents or character. Affiliated descriptions such as 'A wild wind of a beer blowing rich and robust flavours through every sip' provide impressions by association and stray into the vocabulary of wine marketing. This is not to say that such beers lack character or quality, and it is perfectly valid to name beers by imagery or even numerically to receive recognition and acclaim. However, if you are looking for a theme to focus your brewing, developing a style range is a good challenge that is likely to grow and grow.

Fig. 7.5   Example bottles of traditional beer styles.

BREWING NUTRITIONAL BEERS

Increasing awareness of the impact of alcohol on health has led to a rise in popularity of non-alcoholic and low-alcohol beers. Nutritionally focused beers are similarly promoted, particularly gluten-free beers, but novel beers have recently appeared using probiotic and prebiotic components. Such beers have technical challenges, but can be rewarding to trial while providing for colleagues requiring such speciality drinks.

Low-Alcohol Beers

There are two ways of brewing low-alcohol beers. One method is to brew the beer normally and remove the alcohol using technology. This can be by using low-temperature vacuum distillation, which distils alcohol away from the beer at lower temperatures using a low-pressure system. The other technique uses a reverse osmosis method by forcing water and alcohol through a special membrane under high pressure, then diluting the retentive liquid with oxygen-free water. Both of these approaches are expensive and require a great deal of equipment and skill. As such, they will be out of reach to the craft and home brewer.

Low-alcohol beers can be brewed by the home brewer using several different techniques. Mashing the malt between 75 and 80°C, instead of the usual 62–70°C, will inactivate the amylase enzymes and produce fewer fermentable sugars, and so create less alcohol. Diluting a normal beer with oxygen-free liquor will dilute both the alcohol and flavour, but body can be provided by the addition of non-fermentable dextrin. Hop character and bitterness lost by dilution can be enhanced by hop oils and post-fermentation bitterness. Some brewers are fermenting wort by using special yeasts that do not ferment normal brewing sugars. Examples of these yeasts are *Saccharomycodes ludwigii* and *Torulaspora delbrueckii* and are active areas of research.

A word of warning when producing low-alcohol beers is that there are a great many residual sugars left in the beer, so your hygiene practices must be of a high order to prevent unwanted fermentation by contaminants. This could result in a dangerous over-carbonation of the beer.

Gluten-Free Beers

Gluten-free beers are a specialist beer brewed to remove the protein hordein, which can lead to Coeliac disease symptoms. This protein is found in cereals, particularly wheat and barley. If you want to brew a beer with reduced levels of hordein, you have two options. First, you can brew a beer using cereals that do not contain this protein. Rice, maize, buckwheat, sorghum and quinoa can provide a source of carbohydrate for yeast to ferment without hordein. However, there are several issues when using these cereals. One is that some have little or no amylases, or have amylase enzymes that are denatured above 60°C. Quite a few have starch granules that require elevated temperatures to gelatinize or liquify the starch, often above 70°C. Artificial heat and tolerant enzymes must be provided to convert the starch into fermentable sugars. These cereals also have limited quantities of husk, so filtration of the wort run-off can be an issue. This leads to a difficult brewing regime.

An alternative and simpler method of producing gluten-free beer is to add a protease enzyme such as Brewers Clarex at the beginning of fermentation at a rate of 1g per 33ltr. This enzyme reduces the levels of the offending protein by simply digesting it to less reactive peptides.

One word of warning on the production of these beers. Coeliac disease is a serious illness and it is advised to check that levels after digestion are below the legal limit of 20mg/ltr (ppm). Commercial brewers must have their beer checked by a suitable laboratory to ensure that it is eligible to be labelled gluten free, so be cautious about making claims if offering your product.

BREWING HISTORICAL BEERS

It would be easy to say that brewing historical beers should commence with the earliest known Egyptian brews. However, these are particularly difficult to authenticate due to the limited descriptions of processing. They are also likely to differ extensively from what we would recognize today as acceptable beverages due to the ingredients used and the microbiology prevalent in fermentation.

Instead, it is safer, and more relevant, to start with beers from the golden age of brewing when modern brewing technology was introduced, a period when hops were established as essential ingredients and when marketing was not the main driver of sales. In effect, this covers the years 1880 to 1914. During this time, brewers had developed an understanding of the reactions occurring in the mash tun, had identified yeast as the agent of fermentation and had established quality-control laboratories. In addition,

the beer trade involved both a rapid turnover for routine beers and long storage for maturation of stronger, higher-quality ales.

This is not to say that all beer from that period was perfect and examples are recorded of microbial and chemical contamination faults, even resulting in fatalities. However, it is likely that many good, full-flavoured pints were enjoyed as a result of high-quality ingredients and mixed-yeast fermentations. For the home brewer, reproducing or even resurrecting such beers is a complex challenge involving translation of recipes from past units of measurement, interpretation of historical brewing processes and potentially unusual microbial fermentations. Taking these in turn, here are some details and directions to consider.

Translating Recipes

Historical recipes are not easy to find. Many disappeared as breweries closed and production records were discarded, in deference to financial accounts and business legers. Nevertheless, some brewers retained copies, while other brewing books passed to museums. Today, many UK brewery archives are lodged with the National Brewery Centre archives in Burton upon Trent and the Scottish Brewing Archive Association in Glasgow, although records also exist in local authority deposits. These latter sources have the greatest potential for novel finds, as the national archives are well documented. Historical recipes may also be found online in specialist brewing circle websites. See the reference listing in Appendix V for examples.

Once found, it may be difficult to determine whether a recipe has potential for use. In some cases, the details may refer to systems unique to the brewery with no code for translation. Volumes or temperatures may be assumed and not specified, while ingredients may be named colloquially. Even with extensive detail available various difficulties present when deciphering a recipe, particularly in translating units of volume and weight. For example, take the following recipe for a strong XXXX beer from the Hammond's Brewery in Bradford, 15 May 1903 – a copy of which is available in Appendix I.

Table 7.1 Hammond's XXXX Beer Recipe

Malts

Black	½	X 50	25
Yorkshire	14½	X 90	1,305
Chilian	7	X 82	574
Foreign	5	X 82	410
Maize	5	100	500
Inv No. 2	7	70	490
Total	**39**		**3,304**

Hops

Smith MK 01	84	2.5hrs
Brand SX 02	84	2.5hrs
Bavarian 02	84	Sparge

First, the units used in the malt list are quarters, a historic measure based on volume. One quarter translates to 336lb, or 152.4kg. This recipe has a total of 39 quarters, or 5,944kg.

The second value specified is the extract of a quarter of each malt in units of brewer's pounds. Brewer's pounds are the pounds of extract per barrel of 36gal – in effect, the excess weight when filled with wort compared to when filled with water. Brewer's pounds can be converted to gravity by multiplying by 2.73. This can be applied to each malt, so the Yorkshire pale malt is 14.5 quarters (2,210kg) with an extract value of $90 \times 2.73 = 542,948L°$ in total. The brew sheet indicates that 133.5 barrels of wort was collected = $133.5 \times 164 = 21,894$ltr. The Yorkshire pale malt thus contributes $542,948/21,894 = 24.8$ degrees of gravity to the wort. This calculation can be applied to the weights of the other malts and their extract specifications combined to produce a final wort gravity of 1062.8.

You can use this figure as the target fermentation gravity or attenuation, although the recipe sheet does not specify the target finishing gravity. This, however, can be seen from the fermentation record, which plots the gravity, in brewer's pounds, each day. Interestingly, the brew was fermented in four separate fermenters, numbers 18, 19, 20 and 24, indicating a mismatch between brew volume and fermenter capacity.

Finishing gravities for these four ferments were 5.4, 5.4, 5.4 and 5.8 brewer's pounds respectively. On average, the finishing gravity of the beer when blended would be 1.015°. The final alcohol would thus be (62.8-15) $\times 0.131 = 6.3\%$ABV, with gravity contributions of 0.48, 24.8, 10.9, 7.8, 9.5 and 9.3 respectively from the individual malts.

The hop contribution is more difficult to interpret because varieties are not specified. In fact, the names given are for farms or hop factors, as this recipe is before hop varieties were identified. There is, nevertheless, some information provided in the MX and SC initials, which stand for mid Kent and Sussex respectively. Since these brews are Edwardian and before intensive breeding, the nearest contemporary hop varieties are probably best assumed to be Fuggles, with a low bitterness. Today, Fuggles would be around 5.0% α acid, but it may be better to assume a level of half of this prior to breeding programmes and to allow for much of the hop being added late in the boil. Assuming an extraction efficiency of 35% (similar to small-scale production today), the bitterness contribution of the 252lb (114.3kg) would provide a BU of 45.7.

Historical Brewing Processes

Other brewing features available in historical recipes may include liquor treatments, mash temperatures, fermentation temperatures and, occasionally, an indication of yeast handling. During the 1880–1918 period, standard production technology would be used with good mixing of liquor and grist through Steel's Mashers, isothermal mash temperature control, steam boiling and fermentation cooling. Today's production techniques would thus be applicable. Interestingly, many breweries from this period used copper vessels (*see* Figure 2.7a&b).

Yeast strain selection, however, would be more uncertain, as mixed strains would be common and these provide a broader range of flavours and fermentation management, for example in flocculation to produce clarity. Sourcing such yeasts is difficult, but it is acknowledged that the more revered stock ales were matured with *Brettanomyces* yeasts to produce more complex flavours. Strains of *Brettanomyces* may be obtained from yeast suppliers and would be worth including if maturing your beers for some months.

Brewing beers from other historical periods is also possible on a small scale – and in fact was conducted years ago when brewing at home, in farms and in small communities was routine. Two other periods to consider are medieval brewing before hops were introduced and monastic brewing. These periods do overlap, but will have difference sources of record.

Medieval brewing was distinctive in the use of herbs for flavour instead of hops and so providing very different beers, commonly termed ales. Sweet gale, wormwood, tansy and yarrow are example herbs used and offer extensive opportunities to develop novel beer flavours. Limited records are available to indicate proportions of each, so experimentation will be needed. A further complication is that the common term gruit may be interpreted as simply the mixture of herbs infused in the mash. It is also possible that herbs and spices were mixed with the grist in advance of brewing. This action would allow sugars from flower nectar and fruits to coat the grains and encourage

yeasts and bacteria present to start digestion. As such, the mash may have been partly processed before liquor was added and yeast populations primed for later fermentation.

Such beers would also be more malt-focused in their flavour and likely have a higher finishing gravity with lower alcohol content as yeast management was more limited. Clarity would be poor, but nutrition possibly higher than beers today due to residual yeast and malt components. They might also have good prebiotic and probiotic potential. Nevertheless, their shelf life would be short without hops and care may be needed if brewing them today to prevent over carbonation if unfermented sugars remain at bottling.

Monastic and university brewing has greater potential for sourcing records as institutions would have been better placed to retain documentation, albeit possibly requiring translation from Latin. Some Elizabethan texts describe brewing, for example *The English Housewife* by Gervase Markham in 1615 and *The Closet of the Eminently Learned Sir Kenelme Digbie, Kt., Opened (1669)*. Dedicated brewing books began to appear in the next hundred years and prolifically in the nineteenth century, providing much greater resource of recipes. Figure 7.6. shows a range of popular brewing texts from Victorian times.

A general feature of brewing before hops was that the wort from the mash would not necessarily be boiled but fermented directly, possibly with additions of herb and spice infusions. Reports of production suggest that the mash was mixed with boiling water, which would greatly reduce starch digestion. It is likely that routine drinking beers would be low in alcohol, although those from institutions would include strong beers brewed more carefully for quality and character.

Fig. 7.6   Victorian brewing texts.

Brewing with Unusual Microbial Fermentations

Mention has been made of wild fermentations and of wild yeast, topics of increasing interest to the serous home brewer. Some commercial beers are still produced using natural fermentations without addition of brewing yeast, particularly in Belgium. The features of Belgian Lambic fermentations have been documented and can be emulated if the relevant yeast and bacteria are inoculated. However, leaving wort to ferment naturally carries hazards. Not only are acid-producing bacteria likely to grow, but there is the potential for hazardous pathogens to be present and persist if hops are not used. This risk is low, but would depend on local hygiene and environmental contamination. Brewing in food preparation areas and with possibility of contamination from soil or animals should definitely be avoided.

Finally, to return to ancient ales such as those from the Egyptian or Roman period and to emphasize how these beers may differ from today's. Again, herbs and fruits such as dates are likely to provide the flavouring element, along with wild fermentation of mixed yeast and bacteria. Although revered in their time, these may have been considered a nourishment as well as for any inebriation potential and have a very short shelf life. Recreations of these beers have used wild barley and historical wheat varieties, along with dates and other fruit contributing to their character. This is definitely a forefront area of brewing and one still awaiting further evidence to interpret and experiment.

BREWING TRADITIONAL BEERS OF THE WORLD

Standard beer styles are strongly focused on countries with an industrial history. Many other beers exist around the world, although a large number reflect colonization by European nations and the establishment of their brewery traditions. British, German, French and Dutch brewing influences are prevalent in many parts of the world and today the beers from international breweries are the same wherever you go.

Nevertheless, there are some indigenous beers surviving and providing opportunity to extend your brewing experience. Brewed with a wide range of local ingredients and microorganisms, these beers are only now appearing as options for home brewing. Examples include farmhouse beers from Scandinavia and Umqombothi from South Africa. Here are three to try, although others continue to be promoted as brewers travel and interchange experiences.

Norwegian and Scandinavian Farmhouse Beers/Sahti

Brewing in extreme conditions can lead to extreme beers. In Norway and other parts of Scandinavia, farmhouse beers would be brewed to provide for harsh winter conditions and were often strong and flavoured with juniper. They are traditionally fermented with a robust yeast termed kveik. Studies show that these yeasts are particularly resistant to stresses found in brewing and can produce high alcohol levels up to 12%ABV, or even beyond to 16% for some kveik strains.

Two main styles have been recorded and differ as to whether the wort is boiled or not. Grain ale, or *kornøl*, is a raw ale produced by fermenting unboiled wort directly with kveik yeast. A stronger beer, *heimabrygg*, use boiled wort and can be a version of barley wine.

The features of kveik yeasts are interesting as they produce fruity ester flavours without phenolic off flavours, are highly flocculent and have strong attenuations. Kveik yeasts survive drying better than other yeasts, which allows them to remain dormant between brews when coated on to a collection of juniper branches or carefully carved twisted torus woodwork. Analysis of kveik yeasts indicates a range of genetic diversity but also common genetic heritage, possibly resulting from hybridization among brewing and wild yeasts.

A typical kveik fermentation would use pale malt, but with branches of fresh juniper at the base of the mash tun or with the wort in the copper. Fermentation would be at relatively high temperatures between 30 and 43°C, with a high yeast pitching volume, and so last for only a few days. Smoked malts may be added for more complex flavours. Production conditions may be basic, as shown in Figure 7.7, but would have stimulated kveik yeast to adapt and become predominant.

Fig. 7.7 An example of traditional Norwegian farmhouse brewing equipment.

Traditionally, it is likely that a mixed fermentation would include lactic-acid bacteria, resulting in a sour beer if kept for some time, particularly for *kornøl* styles. *Heimabrygg* styles, however, would be more resilient to souring and have a longer shelf life due to their high alcohol levels. Co-pitching with other yeasts such as Saison or *Brettanomyces* offers further dimensions of experimentation.

Traditional Sorghum Beers: Umqombothi/Dolo

Traditionally processed African opaque beers vary in their processing, but typically use sorghum, millet and wheat as ingredients for small-scale processing. Being unrefined, they are reported to have high levels of nutrients, particularly amino acids, dietary fibre, minerals, vitamins, protein and carbohydrates. As a result, they also have a high calorific content and may be consumed as a source of energy and as a focus in social events. The high nutrient content produced by the yeast fermentation may help to supplement a poor or deficient diet.

Production is typically on a small scale up to 10ltr using basic vessels that can be sterilized. For 7ltr, mix 500g of malted sorghum with 1kg of maize meal and sterile water at room temperature. Stir and leave this for 24 hours to sour. After this time, raise the temperature to 95°C for 70 minutes, cool to 25°C and gently stir in 500g of malted sorghum. Add a standard brewing yeast and look to ferment the extract for 24–48 hours at around 30°C, or alternatively use a kveik yeast.

Mayan Maize Ale

Corn beers were recognized as indigenous to Mesoamerica before the arrival of Spanish adventurers and remain as a regional tradition, albeit to limited extents. Their ancestry has been confirmed by analysis of teeth residues from burial remains in the ancient city of Casas Grandes in northern Mexico. Starch granules remaining on the teeth showed evidence of the changes typical of mashing and fermentation.

Other archaeological investigations have uncovered an extensive brewing complex at Cerro Baúl in southern Peru and evidence of fermented cacao on pottery from Puerto Escondido in northern Honduras, suggesting the inclusion of chocolate ingredients. Maize ales are likely to have been extensive throughout these regions.

Brewing with maize does present difficulties, as the grains lack enzymes to digest starch. In contemporary brewing maize would be added as an adjunct to mashes containing barley and wheat. Records and contemporary accounts document a traditional solution to this problem through the use of human saliva to contribute amylase enzymes. Chewing maize grains and collecting the residue in a fermenting pot would allow starch digestion and microorganisms to ferment a beer. At Puerto Escondido pottery analysis indicated the presence of theobromine, an indication of the presence of a chocolate-flavoured beer.

While a saliva digestion is not recommended for home brewing, Tesgüino corn beer produced in the Yuto-Aztec region provides an easier option of production. Here, corn kernels are sprouted to stimulate some internal starch digestion. After crushing, the mixture is boiled and fermented naturally with wild yeast. Local grasses and herbs may be processed into a paste and added to the ferment for flavouring. Shelf life is short due to low alcohol, bacterial contamination and lack of preservative hops.

BREWING SEASONAL BEERS

Many brewers produce a specialist beer for anniversaries, but seasonal beers are common in the portfolios of commercial breweries and have an antiquity reflecting the impact of seasonal conditions on brewing. This may reflect climatic conditions or the availability of crops and ingredients, or be centred around festivities. Often these were religious and doubtless reflected monastical control, but in even earlier times special beers were brewed to celebrate solstices, such as Jul (Yule) ale associated with Viking traditions.

Before the availability of refrigeration, it was difficult to produce and mature a beer during the warm summer in many parts of the world. Too high a temperature in fermentation would produce undesirable flavours from the yeast and encourage bacteria to grow and spoil the beer. Brewing in continental countries often stopped in late spring, so beer stocks were required to provide for summer drinking. In some cases, strong beers would be stored and diluted to drinking strength.

Another solution to the difficulties of summer brewing was to ferment in caves where temperatures would be lower and more consistent. This, however, poses difficulties for the ale yeast, which ceases to work below 15°C, so leading to stuck fermentations. Lager beers originated with the appearance of the lager yeast *Saccharomyces pastorianus* as a hybrid between the standard ale yeast *Saccharomyces cerevisiae* and the wine yeast, *Saccharomyces eubayanus*. Like wine yeast, lager yeast is able to ferment at low temperatures, below 15°C, and was suitable for such colder conditions.

Saison Beers

A classic seasonable beer is the Saison style. Originating with local French and Belgian farm brewing, Saison beers were produced in the winter and kept for drinking until the next year's harvest. Typically with an ABV of around 6%, Saison beers have a floral, hoppy aroma, a spicy yeast character and high carbonation. In particular, they have a high attenuation and thus a low finishing gravity, which contributes to a light mouthfeel and refreshing character. The low attenuation is due to their traditional yeasts having diastaticus genetics and thus secreting a glucoamylase enzyme during maturation. This enzyme digests some of the residual dextrin sugars, enhancing bitterness and dryness in the finish.

French and Belgian farms varied in the character of their Saison beers, but traditional recipes are available to try. Traditional Saison beers used local six-row winter barley. These would provide high protein and polyphenols to the beer, resulting in a deep colour and a malt astringency. Other grains such as oats, buckwheat and even spelt could be added and contribute to a thicker mouthfeel. Fermentation may have been of mixed yeasts and bacteria providing some sourness. Example Saison yeasts are sold by suppliers, but beware of these contaminating your standard beer yeasts as they will produce over-carbonation and possibly gushing when opening.

Märzenbiers

Another classic seasonal beer is Märzenbier, or Oktoberfest. Like Saisons, Märzenbier was a high-gravity seasonal beer in Bavaria brewed at the end of spring and stored until autumn. Oktoberfest versions were produced traditionally by German breweries to coincide with the Munich Oktoberfest celebration. Initially only those produced by breweries in Munich could enter the Oktoberfest, but today the style is available worldwide and is characterized by a dark copper colour and mild hop flavour, in effect an amber lager and so requiring a lager yeast for fermentation. Earlier versions may have used crystal

Fig. 7.8   German drinking pots.

UK Seasonal Beers

While the UK has benefited from a less extreme brewing climate through the year, it also has a strong history of seasonal beers. As in many countries, this is demonstrated by the prevalence of pale ales in summer and darker ales in winter, but also celebratory beers at festivals. Many UK breweries have specialized in winter ales with pungently rich and spicy flavours and strong alcohol levels.

Historically brewed in October with the first hops of the year, winter beers would be strong in alcohol and have a long maturation time. Initially associated with country house brewing, they were incorporated into commercial brewery portfolios and often promoted as Christmas ales or Winter Warmers. Examples of some ingredients are shown in Figure 7.9.

SOME EXPERIMENTS

Who knows what beers will be popular in ten years' time, in twenty years or beyond? The pace of brewing innovation is moving rapidly, along with drinkers' preferences. Marketing beers is increasingly difficult as fashions and expectations alter so quickly. For the home brewer, these pressures are muted but still present. It is difficult to anticipate, but here are some major areas of innovation and research today. Not all may appear as beers for sale, but they do offer some prospects of development even on a small scale.

and Munich malts to produce a darker beer with more malt-focused character. Drinking from heavy glass or stone pots as shown in Figure 7.8 would contribute to the character of the beer.

Enhanced and Modified Hop Extracts

For many years beers were only brewed with whole hop cones, carefully dried and stored through the seasons. Hop pellets appeared in the 1950s and provided savings in storage, ease of use and an alteration to boiling systems. Oil extracts soon followed and are commonly used in large-scale brewing. On a small scale, pellets and oils are difficult to manage

Fig. 7.9   Winter ale ingredients and example bottle.

as the powder from pellets causes haze and oil is very concentrated, making measurement to the boil difficult. Hop cones are easier to manage, but suppliers are looking at ways to enhance their contribution to bitterness and aroma, particularly in late hopping and dry hopping. Experimentation in these areas is of interest by combining different varieties, particularly if home-grown. The inclusion of hops after fermentation has been a subject of investigation, as enzymes may be released from the hops to change flavours and potentially digest residual sugars.

Another strand of interest is to determine whether other parts of the hop plant or other herbs can be used as well as the cones. Hop leaves and even stalks may provide some, and possibly different, hop flavours, which could be worth exploring either from direct addition or as infusions.

Cask Aging

Maturing beers in spirit or wine casks is increasingly practised by commercial brewers and does have potential for home brewing. One hundred years ago all beer would have been stored and matured in wood casks, but more recently stainless-steel predominates. Studies have shown the wide range of flavours that arise from wood and which transfer to whisky, wine and beer. Commercial breweries are increasingly keen to promote these for their effects and as marketing potential. Although a wooden cask as shown in Figure 7.10a is an ideal and traditional approach to achieve

Fig. 7.10b   Wood chips.

a wood input, it is not essential as wood chips shown in Figure 7.10b can be added to your beer to similar effect. Three to six months of maturation will provide a good extraction and clear flavour effect, but look out for different woods and different treatments including smoking for peaty flavours and soaking in spirits to extract more complex contributions.

Beers with Benefits

Historically, beer was regularly promoted for health benefits, even by the medical profession, and was provided to patients in hospitals. This is nowadays recognized as inappropriate, considering the hazards of alcohol, but beer, nevertheless, contains many beneficial nutrients such as vitamins and fibre. In past times, beer would have been served with its indigenous yeasts and would potentially contain probiotics. Today, breweries are seeking to combine low-alcohol beer with sources of specific nutrients and produce nutraceutical drinks. For example, a medicinal plant, *Parastrephia lucida*, from South America has been incorporated into the brewing of a Porter beer with enhanced antioxidant capacity. Similarly, goji berries have been used in beers to enhance levels of the flavonoid rutin and propolis extract, collected

Fig. 7.10a   Wooden casks.

by bees, used to increase antioxidant activities. It is unlikely that standard beer can be promoted as a nutritional aid, but low-alcohol versions have potential and may be worth considering in small-scale experiments.

Cultivate Some Mushrooms

Yeasts are well known as fungi, but they are not the only ones to grow on wort. Many other fungi, particularly edible species, will grow on spent grain and can make a tasteful contribution to your kitchen. Disposing of spent grain from the mash is easy on a small scale, as it can be composted with general food waste. Commercial brewers have a more difficult challenge, typically donating to cattle or poultry feed. However, a number are now using spent grain to produce valuable additions of edible fungi to their product range.

Inoculating a spent grain and sawdust mixture with pure culture of fungal mycelium is an alternative use that can lead to a good harvest of edible mushroom caps. Mushroom suppliers can provide suitable growbags and inoculations and given the right temperature control, your incubations will produce edible fungi within a few weeks. The oyster fungus, *Pleurotus ostreatus* (*see* Figure 7.11) is the most chosen species, but a variety of others are available with different flavours and potential to vary your stir fry as you enjoy any of the fine beers you have developed skills to produce.

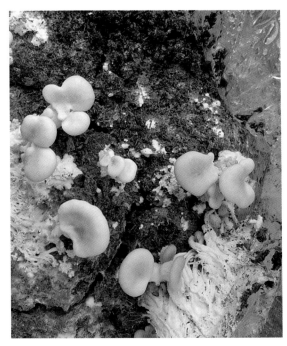

Fig. 7.11 Oyster mushrooms growing on brewery spent grain.

CHAPTER 8

TESTING AND MAINTAINING BEER QUALITY

Defining a quality beer is both a profession and a common topic of discussion in pubs. Professionally, rigorous analyses document the levels of specific chemical, physical and microbiological components of a beer, match these against targets and pronounce judgements as to a beer's saleability. In contrast, discussion in a pub or bar is mostly subjective, will vary from person to person and be susceptible to daily variations of meals taken, time of day, general mood, as well as the tone of the conversation. It is no surprise that these two approaches to quality do not always agree.

For the home brewer this has less impact. This is partly because the extent of laboratory analysis will be limited, but also because the drinking audience is likely to be more receptive – and forgiving – of mistakes. Nevertheless, it is worth having some degree of analysis and recording, so as to guide future production – in effect, a basic quality system to which you can refer, not least so that an outstanding beer can be reproduced to the same standard.

While some basic laboratory procedures can be applied to home production, the one technique that unites analysis and personal response is tasting. Naturally this is a major purpose of your home production, but it is also a technique incorporated into laboratory analysis, albeit in very controlled protocols. Tasting in the bar, or at home with your well-crafted beers, has less focus on identifying specific flavours but does include overall impressions, which provide critical feedback not always addressed in small-sip laboratory tastings.

The following sections address the techniques used in testing your beers for chemical, microbiological and flavour analysis, providing guidance on the value and relevance of each test. Many of the laboratory procedures are likely to be too expensive to develop at home, but are worth obtaining from a commercial laboratory for occasional or problem brews. Tasting, however, is a skill you can develop progressively to provide some valuable information during the brew and on the final beer. It will also give you skills to contribute to tasting panels for home-brew competitions and, possibly, professional beers.

CHEMICAL ANALYSIS

Chemical analysis of beer can be an expensive and specialist process. The degree of analysis depends on how much you can afford and how attracted you are to laboratory activities. The following section looks at simple procedures that can be conducted at home and then provides details of how these are conducted with laboratory equipment.

Home-Based Analysis
Alcohol Level   As you are not selling your beer, it is not essential to have a highly accurate measurement of your beer's alcohol level. It is, nevertheless, a valuable check to determine how well your beer matches the recipe. For a home brewer, the basic

Fig. 8.1   Iodine test on mash samples showing positive (black) and negative (brown) staining.

analysis of alcohol by volume can be achieved using a suitable saccharometer and measuring the specific gravity at 20°C, at the beginning and end of fermentation and applying the relevant F-factor (*see* Appendix II).

Starch   The simple iodine test is a cheap and straightforward way to decide if starch has been converted to sugars. This will confirm that your mash has been effective and would be tested on a small sample towards the end of the mash. Either take a sample of grains and soak in a few drops of iodine solution, or place in a test tube with iodine. A black staining of the grains indicates that starch is still present, while digested grains will stain brown as shown in Figure 8.1. Be careful with iodine, as spillage into the brew will mean a discard due to iodine's toxicity.

pH   A pH meter can be bought for less than £100, but it will lack the reliability of a more expensive instrument. Knowing the pH of your worts and beers can help you to understand the process, but it is a luxury for the home brewer and will need constant calibration.

Minerals   Salts in your brewing water can be analysed by adding Palintest tablets, which react with and indicate levels of a particular salt. Such a test can cover the specific salts in brewing liquor, but to cover the range can cost upward of £100.

Laboratory Analysis

A purpose-built brewing laboratory costs tens, if not hundreds, of thousands of pounds to equip. It also requires skilled and dedicated staff to ensure that the results are accurate and reproducible. What chemical analyses are typically applied to commercial beer?

ABV   Alcohol by volume is measured by various techniques. Distillation of beer is a tried and tested method and one approved by HMRC (HM Revenue & Customs), but other techniques can be used. Measuring the refractive index together with the density of the beer can give alcohol levels and machines can do this automatically. The density meter can give you the present gravity of the beer.

Colour   Colour is measured using a comparative disc or ideally a spectrophotometer, but for the home brewer using your eye together with a suitable colour chart is good enough, although be aware of difficulties if you are colour blind.

Clarity   Clarity of a beer can be seen with the human eye and is good enough for a home brewer. In a brewing laboratory there are analyses that can put a value on the haze level. Specific analysis of proteins and polyphenols can predict how quickly a beer will develop haze over time.

Foam   Foam potential can be measured, indicating how long a beer head will last. A target half-life is 95 seconds under controlled conditions of gas injection. A crude test is possible if you can standardize a pour into a measuring cylinder, but is difficult to make consistent.

Bitterness   Bitterness requires an extraction method using an organic solvent, then measuring the extraction fluid in a spectrophotometer with ultraviolet wavelength illumination. The bitterness figure is expressed as EBU (European Bitterness Unit) and mg/ltr of iso-alpha acid. Tasting will be the best approach for home brew, ideally using standard commercial beers for comparison.

Carbon Dioxide   Carbon-dioxide levels can be determined through measuring the pressure and temperature of a beer. The container is pierced to get the measurement, then, using a calculation based on Henry's law of gases, the CO_2 value is given. These machines can cost £1,000. Other methods require instruments costing over £10,000 using infrared technology. These machines can also measure oxygen levels in beer. Elevated levels of oxygen in beer can, over time, cause hazes to develop, along with paper or cardboard flavours.

Flavour Components   Gas chromatographs can measure diacetyl or butterscotch flavours in beer and HPLC (High-Pressure Liquid Chromatography) can measure the different hop compounds. These are clearly beyond the scope of home brewing, for which it is best to rely on flavour analysis against reference samples. For example, the bitterness level of standard Carling is 9.5EBU, Tetley original bitter is 18EBU and Old Tom strong ale 25EBU.

Certain specialist laboratories will be needed to measure components such as gluten levels for gluten-free beers, ATNC (nitrosamine compound, which is a potential carcinogen) and heavy metals. In general, a large commercial brewing laboratory should be able to do the following tests:

- original gravity
- present gravity
- alcohol by volume
- pH and acidity

- haze and predictive haze
- foam potential
- bitterness (EBU)
- colour (EBC)
- CO_2 and DO_2.

Although this analysis section may seem daunting to a home brewer, you can be assured that you and your fellow drinkers certainly do not need to do all of these. The perception of beer is based on your senses, meaning that visual and flavour senses will lead you to that good beer experience. Look carefully at the beer you produced for clarity and colour. See the nature of the bubbles and how the foam stays in the glass. Smell and taste the beer, be critical and record your and other people's thoughts.

As noted already, the parameters that the home brewer really should record and calculate are the original gravity and final gravity, then calculate the alcohol content using F-factor tables. In a world where there are laws about operating machinery and in particular driving, knowing your alcohol intake may well protect you from breaking those laws. Also, it is important for health reasons to be aware of and manage your alcohol intake.

If, as a home brewer, you need to have your beer analysed, you are far better off sending your beer to a specialist laboratory such as Brewlab, who will give you a prompt, accurate idea of the important physical parameters.

MICROBIOLOGY ANALYSIS AND HURDLES TO MICROBIAL GROWTH

As has been mentioned in previous chapters, microbiology is critical to controlling the quality of your beers. The best production skills can be easily ruined by a chance contamination with bacteria or wild yeast. Brewing at home is more liable than commercial brewing to incur accidental and opportunistic contamination, as homes have many other activities that would not be allowed in industrial premises. Stored foods, cooking activities, pets and even children may all transmit contamination into your beer. That said, only certain sources are likely to carry the specific microbes that will cause brewing issues, so it is important to identify and control these.

All foods have ingredients that can encourage or discourage microbial growth and although some dried foods can last for decades, all foods eventually become inedible and decompose. The target of the food industry is to achieve a suitable shelf life as required by the distribution chain. For some foods such as bread and milk this shelf life may be as short as a few days, while for tinned foods it can be years.

Beer has a shelf life, but defining this is more difficult than a food like milk where off flavours are clear to everyone. Beer can be stable for some time and only deteriorate slowly, making it difficult to judge when it should be rejected. Even then, some old beer can be acclaimed by drinkers for its maturity and complexity. Fortunately, beer resists growth by pathogens and is generally unlikely to be poisonous. This does, though, depend on strength and weaker low-alcohol beers are most likely to show deterioration and require more attention to maintain their quality.

As with all food production, the shelf life of beer is a function of its features and how those can resist the growth of contaminants. Shelf life in beer is prolonged by several key components, each of which may be considered a hurdle to microbial growth. Of these, alcohol and acid provide two major impacts. Both act as toxins to microbes, inhibiting growth and killing cells. Together they provide a powerful deterrent to

Fig. 8.2   Surface pellicle on beer.

microbes, particularly standard food pathogens such as *E. coli* and *Salmonella*.

Other components assist in this inhibition. Hops, for example, have specific toxins that kill many bacteria. Low levels of sugars and nitrogen compounds are additional hurdles to microbial growth, while the absence of oxygen will stop many other microbes, including some such as the acetic-acid bacteria, which require oxygen to grow.

The more hurdles present in a food, the harder it is for microbes to spoil. Following the standard brewing procedures will produce a beer with a sound range of hurdles, with the potential for a long shelf life of months in a bottle. Draught beer is a little less secure once serving commences, as oxygen may be introduced and the dispensing pipework may harbour microbes, which can feed into the container.

A major area to be aware of is the effect of changing any of the standard hurdle protections, for example lowering hop levels, having low levels of alcohol or high levels of residual sugar. Such beers may be more liable for spoilage and require greater hygiene control – or, of course, drinking early.

'BAD BUGS'

What then are the microbes to be aware of and how can they be avoided? A number of these have been mentioned in previous chapters, but following is a brief list with background details.

Wild Yeasts

Brewing yeasts are acceptable in your final beer as they will assist with carbonation and provide maturation of flavours. Wild yeast may certainly contribute to carbonation, often extensively, but their flavours are likely to be undesirable. Many produce phenolic characteristics, making beer taste medicinal, particularly if any chlorinated water enters the wort. Wild yeast may not settle as well as brewing yeast, leaving beer cloudy. It may also produce a surface pellicle (*see* Figure 8.2), which is unattractive and looks messy in a glass.

Perhaps the most undesirable effect of wild-yeast contamination is from those species that can ferment

Fig. 8.3   A gushing beer.

dextrin sugars. These diastaticus yeasts produce an enzyme that digests the dextrins, releasing fermentable sugars. This normally takes some months, as the effect is often slow, but the carbon dioxide produced from this additional fermentation may cause your beer to gush when opened, like that shown in Figure 8.3, or, in the worst condition, explode. Home brewing is beset with a reputation for poor management of secondary condition in bottles and subsequent explosions. The addition of wild yeast to the mix is clearly a reputation to avoid.

Lactic-Acid Bacteria (LAB)

Lactic-acid bacteria are not always regarded with dismay and distaste. They are fundamental in the production of many fermented foods, such as yoghurt, sauerkraut, kimchi and so on, through their production of lactic acid. In beer, however, this is undesirable and typically a fault – excepting, of course, in sour beers.

Lactic-acid bacteria can survive and grow without oxygen and are thus a danger throughout the brewing process. Once present, they are able to grow rapidly and sour a beer to a low pH and an acid level that distracts from all the other flavours you have striven to generate. Short of pasteurization to kill everything in the beer, it is impossible to stop their growth and a beer contaminated with LAB should be discarded – safely and without contaminating your brewing environment.

It appears that lactic-acid bacteria have evolved to grow in the same environments in which brewing yeast have evolved, that is, rich, high-sugar solutions. In nature, they would co-exist, but in your brew it is essential to separate your yeast from LAB. To achieve this, keep your yeast stocks and cultures in very clean containers (see Figure 8.4) and avoid exposure to environments where they can be contaminated. Malt dust, for example, contains plenty of LAB, so don't open your yeast when mashing-in.

Lactic-acid bacteria have also evolved the ability to resist the antibacterial effect of hops. This effect is due to the α acids and iso-α acids, which can damage the bacteria cell membranes. Lactic-acid bacteria can export these acids rapidly, so limiting their effect, and they are thus hop-resistant. The sour taste of lactic acid is a good indicator of contamination, but other flavours

Fig. 8.4   Brewing yeast stored securely.

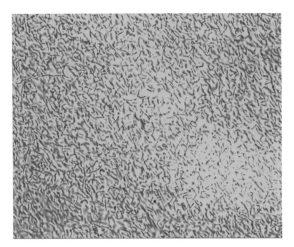

Fig. 8.5a Microscopic appearances of lactic-acid bacteria cells.

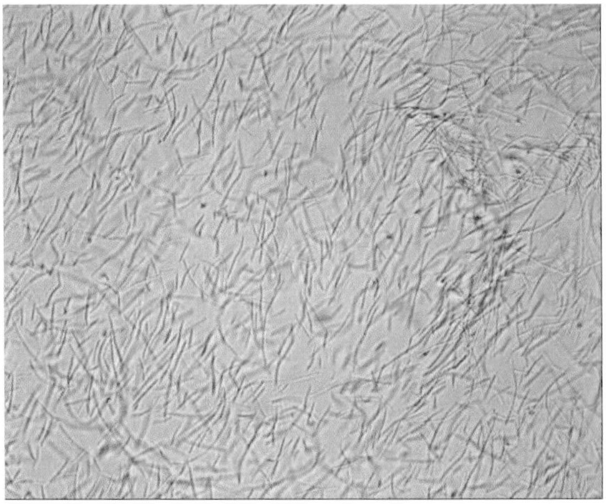

Fig. 8.5b Different microscopic appearances of lactic-acid bacteria cells.

are also produced, diacetyl in particular, but in some cases dimethyl sulphide. Check for aromas of a suspect beer as an indication, although a microscope view will be definitive. For reference, an example view of lactic-acid bacteria cells is shown in Figures 8.5a&b.

Acetic-Acid Bacteria (AAB)

The acetic-acid bacteria are distinctive by their production of acetic acid – in effect vinegar – so making your beer highly unpalatable, even as a sour beer. Unlike lactic-acid bacteria, they require oxygen to grow, so are less hazardous during the brewing process. However, if your beer is contaminated at packaging and contains a certain amount of air, such as in underfilled bottles, they are likely to grow and ruin a good product.

Acetic-acid bacteria also colonize brewing equipment, tubing in particular, so good cleaning is essential throughout. Like wild yeast, they often grow at the surface of beer where oxygen levels are highest, forming a pellicle and plenty of acetic acid. Other flavours are often associated with growth, along with turbidity and surface biofilm within tubing.

USING A MICROSCOPE

Microscopes are not always used in commercial breweries. Not because of their expense, but because

a certain level of skill and experience is needed to process the sample and make interpretations. Small breweries relying on just a few staff may lack the training required. This may not apply to home brewing, where time may be available to develop skills – or where these have been remembered from school or college.

A suitable quality microscope would cost in the region of £200–£500 and include the following features listed below and shown in Figure 8.6:

- **sturdy construction:** keeps the lenses in alignment
- **internal illumination:** provides the correct colour and level of light entering the lenses
- **condenser lens:** focuses light on the sample and should have a focus control
- **iris diaphragm:** controls the light level and is situated below the condenser
- **mechanical stage:** holds the sample stable and has controls to move the slide smoothly
- **objective lenses:** 10× and 40× lens will provide suitable magnification; 100× is not necessary and will not provide more useful detail
- **eyepiece lenses:** binocular 10× magnification eyepieces will provide a final magnification of 100× and 400× from your objectives.

For serious use, it is worth investing in an eyepiece

camera so that you can record images of your yeast, beer and so on, and integrate these with your brewing records.

TASTING YOUR BEERS

By now, you will have generated a wealth of experience tasting the beers you have produced and, hopefully, many will have attracted acclaim from friends, family and colleagues. Referring back to the different approaches of laboratory tasting and home or pub/bar tasting, following is some guidance to help you develop skills in flavour identification and application to quality assessment.

First, a look at your tasting apparatus – your nose and tongue. These are some of the most sensitive parts of the sensory system and most regularly used. When young, these are particularly responsive to food flavours and to the air you smell. However, because of limited experience, it is difficult to recognize and identify specific flavours. With time and training, this becomes more accurate and can be directed to assessing your beer.

Fig. 8.6   An optical microscope suitable for brewery use.

Maintaining Tasting Physiology

The sensory surfaces in the nose and tongue contain numerous receptors and neurones to carry impulses to the brain for interpretation. These receptors can be blunted if overstimulated, or if coated with food and mucus, so a clean mouth and blown nose put them in their best condition. Colds and other infections also interfere with the sensory response, so it is best not to rely on tasting until these have worked out of your system. Recent foods also impact on responses. Spicy foods particularly, but anything very strongly flavoured will have an impact for an hour or two, so the best time for tasting is typically late morning or late afternoon.

Maintaining the Tasting Environment

The place where you taste can have a large impact on your flavour perception and impression of a beer. Visual, aroma and aural distractions enhance or reduce your sensitivity and change your overall response, particularly if tasting with others who may influence your personal view. Nevertheless, tasting as a panel is great for training and putting your impressions in context.

For accurate assessment of your beer, taste in a neutral environment with no interfering smells or noise. Take deep sniffs initially, then a mouthful. Cover all of your tongue, then swallow before finalizing your response, as taste receptors are present in the throat as well as the mouth. For a full flavour profile, look to identify specific malt flavours, malty, caramel and roast, as well as hop aromas, bitterness, fruitiness from yeast and additional flavours from maturation and novel ingredients. A tasting kit of common beer flavours will help to

Table 8.1   Beer Flavour Associations

Flavour	Easily Available Comparison
Malty	Fresh pale malt in warm water
Caramel	Crystal malt in warm water
Roast	Black malt and roast barley in warm water
Bitterness	Boiled extract of hops
Hop aroma	Fresh hops
Fruitiness	Various fresh fruits, such as apple, apricot, pineapple, orange; extracts are available in catering sections of shops
Diacetyl	Butterscotch
Dimethyl sulphide	Cabbage, Brussels sprouts
Sulphur	Fresh boiled eggs; struck match
Medicinal	Germolene
Acidic	Vinegar
Astringency	Strong cup of tea

identify these accurately, but the associations in Table 8.1 will provide some guidance.

While tasting, look for the time profile from initial aroma to taste and aftertaste (flavours still apparent after 2 minutes). A scoring sheet will allow you to produce a profile, such as the flavour wheel shown in Figure 8.7a&b, and to compare beers together. As well as profiling your beer, look for specific faults. Acidity is an important indicator of microbial spoilage, along with sulphur and medicinal flavours. A strong astringency indicates problems with sparging control extracting too much tannin from malt, while a high DMS aroma suggests incomplete boiling.

KEEPING RECORDS

It is essential that records of your brews are made and kept. For a commercial brewer, these are needed not

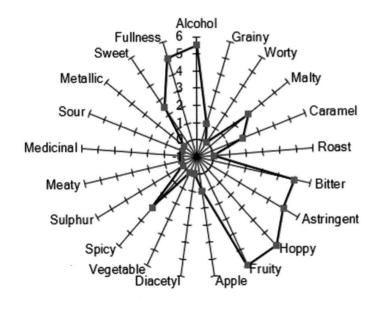

Fig. 8.7a   Example IPA and stout profiles.

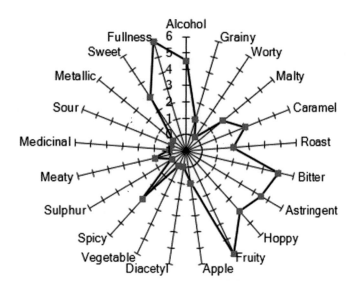

Fig. 8.7b Profiles on a beer flavour wheel.

only for quality-control aspects, but are required by Revenue officials as evidence for tax collection. For the home brewer, they allow for analysis of your efforts and reminders of what you have achieved so that you can make improvements. They also help in planning your brew and reminding you what to do and in what order, enabling the brew to be carried out in a methodical way.

Figures 8.8a, b & c are examples of a recipe sheet written in an Excel format. They relate to the recipe given previously for a blonde beer. By experience, using a spreadsheet format has proved to be the best system, as it can be altered easily and adapted to your needs. Calculations can be incorporated into the spreadsheet and using the copy and paste format recipe forms can be generated quickly. Each recipe can be saved for reuse later. By using a suffix of the brew date on the spreadsheet file, you can keep an electronic reference to build up a library of recipes without the worry of losing sheets of paper. For example, saving the spreadsheet illustrated as C: /Blonde230923 would keep a record of that brew made on 23 September 2023.

Printing out a recipe is often prudent, as invariably due to the nature of brewing it is much more convenient to jot the figures down using a pen with the recipe attached to a clipboard. The example given here is not definitive, but as an idea of how a record sheet can be built up. If you have the computer skills, you can design one that fits your own circumstances. The document consists of several parts.

Malt and Sugar Grist including Liquor Treatment

Grist   This lists the various malts, adjuncts and sugars needed to make up the recipe and the quantities of each. Although not illustrated, in this example it may also include the extract potential of each ingredient so that the percentage extract can be determined. Some professional brewers even include each ingredient batch number to ensure traceability if problems occur. The salts or any other water treatment chemicals are also put in this section. The paper ensures that as the grist is physically made up, each material can be ticked off or initialled to remind you that it has been added as you go through the recipe process.

Mashing   The next part of the recipe takes you through the mashing stage, indicating set points and boxes for recording times and temperatures throughout the brew. It also includes liquor volumes to achieve the correct mashing ratio. Recording times acts as a reminder to do things at the correct stage. The iodine test is a useful technique to determine if the starch has all been converted to sugar. Starch turns

THE HOME BREWER

BLONDE ALE RECIPE & BREW SHEET

DATE 27th September 2023	FV 1
Volume 25 litres	BREW No. 15

MALT & SUGAR GRIST		
Ingredients	Metric	ADDED/Batch Number
Pale Ale Malt	2 Kg	
Cara Gold	450 g	
Pilsner Malt	1.6 Kg	
LIQUOR TREATMENT		
Sodium Bicarbonate (add to HLT)	1.7 g	
Calcium Chloride Flaked (add to malt grist)	7.8 g	
Calcium Sulphate (add to malt grist)	17.9 g	

MASHING				
Mash In Start Time			Set Points	ACTUAL
Mash In End Time		Liquor Temp	73 to 74 ° C	
Stand Time	1 hour	Mash Liquor Volume	10 litres	
Iodine Test		Mash Temp	65 ° C	
Start of Run Off Time		Sparge Temp	76 to 77 ° C	

HOP GRIST		
Ingredients	Metric	ADDED /Batch No.
Target Whole Hops (10% alpha) (add to copper before boil)	25 g	
Willamette Whole Hops (11% alpha) (add to copper after boil)	40 g	
First Gold Whole Hops (7% alpha) add to copper after boil	100 g	
Copper Finings - Irish Moss	1 tsp	

BOILING				Actual
Copper Up Time/Volume		Copper Up Gravity	Aim for 35.5°	
Copper Boil Time		Boil for	Aim for 1 hr	
Copper Cast Time/Volume		Copper Cast Gravity	Aim for 39°	

Fig. 8.8a   Example recipe sheets for recording all of your brewing data.

BLONDE ALE RECIPE & BREW SHEET

DATE 27th September 2023	FV 1
Volume 25 litres	BREW No. 15

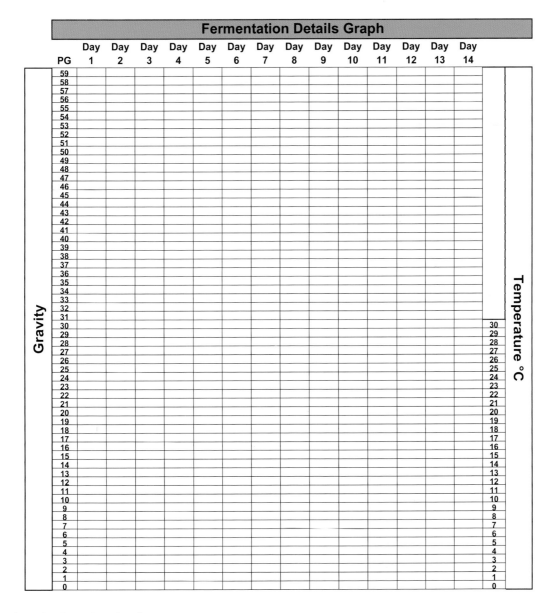

Fig. 8.8b   Example recipe sheet.

THE HOME BREWER

BLONDE ALE RECIPE & BREW SHEET

DATE 27th September 2023	FV 1
Volume 25 litres	BREW No. 15

START OF FERMENTATION ADDITIONS		
Ingredients	Metric	ADDED/Batch No.
Yeast Food	nil	
Yeast Nottingham	17 g	
START OF FERMENTATION DETAILS		
DIP		Gravity (Aim for 1039°)	
LITRES		TEMPERATURE (set point 18 to 20 ° C)	
POST FERMENTATION ADDITIONS		
Ingredients	Metric	Added/Batch No.
Sugar	6.5 g	
RACKING ADDITIONS		
Ingredients	Metric	Added/Batch No.
AUXILLARY FININGS	90 ml	
FININGS (add after auxiliary)	90 ml	
RACKING DETAILS		
DATE		TYPE OF CONTAINER	
NUMBER OF CONTAINERS		BEST BEFORE DATE	

QUALITY PARAMETERS			
ABV	4.20%	PG	1006°
OG	1038°	CO_2	4 g/l

NOTES INCLUDING TASTING NOTES

Fig. 8.8c   Example recipe sheet.

iodine an intense blue/black, while the sugar leaves the iodine its distinctive brown colour. Using a white ceramic tile as a background helps in the iodine test.

Hop Grist   Next is a section to remind you what hops to use and the quantity needed. It should also include batch numbers and α-acid content of the hop, as well as a reminder at what stage of the boiling process to add the hops.

Boiling   This indicates the times for boiling and volumes, as well as the gravity to aim for at the beginning and end of the boil. The evaporation rate can be ascertained by dividing the copper casting gravity by the copper up gravity and expressing this as a percentage; 10% evaporation is a good boil. Gravity set points can be included as target

Start of Fermentation Additions and Details   The next stage of the process covers the addition of yeast, together with the aim points for the start of fermentation. Gravity is a crucial factor at this stage, as this will give you the correct ABV. If your fermenter does not have a volume scale, you could calibrate it yourself by marking volumes with water and a measuring jug, as detailed in the section below on measurements.

Fermentation Details   Measuring the gravity and temperature of the fermentation daily will enable you to keep a check on the performance of the yeast and how the fermentation occurred. This can be used to see any issues. In this example there are two scales, one for temperature and the other for gravity using a saccharometer. It is best to use a different coloured pen for each parameter to distinguish the two scales.

The end of the record sheet can include details of post-fermentation additions, such as clarification agents and priming sugars. It also has a record of what containers are filled and in this example the quality aim points.

An extra box is also included. This is to document any unusual recipe and processing parameters and to add notes. This will help if you want to repeat the recipe. Tasting notes and comments will help you to alter any subsequent recipe to improve the flavour. Include as much information as you want, as any contemporary information will assist in the brewing process after the passage of time.

Measurements   The brewing process does require accurate measuring. There is a minimum of five parameters you need to measure in order to keep good records. Many more can be included, such as the iodine test, but the more you measure the more it will cost you. The following five are a suitable timepiece so that you can accurately record time targets. An alarm function is often a desirable addition.

Weighing scales of a suitable range and accuracy will aid you to measure your ingredient grist. A thermometer will get the vital temperatures correct throughout the brewing process. Gravity measurement, preferably using a saccharometer, is the fourth measurement. A saccharometer over a refractometer is preferred as this can be used both in the brewing and fermentation processes. The final parameter is to have your brewing vessels calibrated for volume. Most home-brewing equipment will have volume scales either etched or scribed, but calibration is easily performed using simple mathematics, so if you find that you must calibrate your HLT, brew kettle or fermenter, following are some tips to do so.

You can measure the volume in your brew equipment by drawing a scale down the side of the vessel or sight glass. You could also take a metric ruler and use this as a dipstick. So how do you go about producing a volumetric scale? If the vessel is a simple cylinder, the relationship is quite simple: volume is $\pi \times$ (diameter/2)$^2 \times$ height.

On a vessel 30cm diameter each cm will be:

- $3.142 \times (30/2)^2 = 3.142 \times 15 \times 15 = 706.95 cm^3$ or $707 cm^3$
- * Since a litre is $10cm \times 10cm \times 10cm = 1,000cm^3$
- * Then every cm is 0.707ltr.

However, brew vessels are never that simply designed, especially near the bottom. The way to get around this is to use a measuring jug and add water until you get on the straight side of the vessel. Record how many litres this is. Then you can apply the principle above, not forgetting to add how much water you used. The vessel can be marked to show the volume if you are using a dipstick and a table can be formulated using a spreadsheet. Alternatively, if you have the patience, you can simply add a litre at a time to the vessel and mark each litre.

TROUBLE-SHOOTING

Identifying problems with a beer typically starts with the taste, but clarity and head formation may also be out of specification. Some problems are immediately evident, but others gradually develop as your beers mature. Identifying the cause of a problem is more difficult and may take some investigation. Records of the brew day and beer measurements can help greatly, but experience is an essential factor. The list in Table 8.2 covers many of the likely causes of problems and suggests solutions you can apply.

Table 8.2   Beer and Brewing Problems with Potential Causes and Possible Solutions

Problem	Symptoms Causes of Issue	Potential Solution	Possible
Fermentation does not start or is sluggish at starting	After one day of fermentation there are no bubbles on the surface of the beer, or only a few bubbles appearing on the surface. The air lock is not bubbling at all or very sporadically	Was the yeast added at the correct time or at all?	Add more yeast with vigorous stirring
		The wort or beer is too cold	Try to warm up the beer and add more yeast
		The wort or beer is too hot at collection, potentially killing the yeast	Add more yeast when the wort is below 23°C and stir in vigorously
		The yeast added may be inactive or beyond its date	Check packet and add another yeast
		Some yeasts are naturally sluggish	Check yeast characteristics on the packet
		Not enough yeast added	Check quantity of yeast against manufacturer's instructions and add more if necessary
Fermentation has stopped too early	After a few days of fermentation, the beer slows down and stops at a saccharometer reading higher than expected	The wort produced has higher levels of non-fermentable sugars than expected	Next brew, check the mashing temperature with a calibrated thermometer
		The beer was unexpectedly chilled	Warm up the beer and add more yeast, stirring vigorously
		The beer is too warm	Cool the beer down and repitch with more yeast, stirring vigorously

Problem	Symptoms Causes of Issue	Potential Solution	Possible
		Not enough nutrients in the wort	Add yeast food, together with more yeast
		Yeast not tolerant to the alcohol produced	Some yeasts simply are not able to ferment strong beers. Try to use a yeast that is suitable to the alcohol you wish to achieve
Beer does not taste right	The beer tastes of vinegar	Contamination by bacteria particularly *Acetobacter*	Check cleanliness
The beer just does not taste the way you wanted. Issues can be many. With bacterial or wild yeast infection, this can be due to poor cleaning and sterilizing of equipment	The beer tastes of green apples	Beer has not been warm-conditioned long enough	Condition or mature for longer until flavour disappears
	The beer tastes of butterscotch	The beer has not been warm-conditioned for long enough after primary fermentation, or *pediococci* bacteria have contaminated the beer	Warm-condition for longer; if no change in flavour check cleanliness
	The beer tastes medicinal or of TCP	Wild-yeast contamination, or using water with chlorine added	Always heat water to drive off chlorine. Check cleanliness
	Beer tastes of lactic acid	Caused by contamination by *Lactobacillus* bacteria	Check cleanliness
	Beer tastes of cooked vegetables such as cabbage	This can be malt-derived, but in extreme cases it can be by *Obesumbacterium* bacteria in the wort	Check cooling procedure post-boiling and add yeast as soon as possible
	Beer tastes rancid, like baby's sick	Caused by leaving the yeast too long in contact with the beer. Dead yeast cells leach very unpleasant flavours	Remove yeast from conditioning beer periodically during maturation
	In the bottle the beer tastes of cardboard or papery	Tiny amounts of oxygen react with beer over time	Eliminate oxygen after fermentation through to bottle filling. Avoid using ferrous material
	Beer tastes metallic or astringent	Many causes, but could be due to using ferrous equipment. Over-sparging your malt in the mash tun can also cause this	Always use stainless steel or plastic materials

Problem	Symptoms Causes of Issue	Potential Solution	Possible
Beer does not clear	The beer after treatment with clarification agents does not go bright	Contamination by bacteria or wild yeast can cause clarity issues, but usually also linked to flavour faults	Check cleanliness
		The clarification agents used are inactive either by poor storage or beyond the best-before date	Check best-before date. Replace with fresh clarification agents
		Starch from the mashing process in grain brewing can cause the haze	Do iodine test at the end if conversion. If positive, check your mashing procedures
		The beer is too cold and has formed a chill haze; the haze goes after warming	Look at chill haze treatment, or temperature of serve too cold
		The yeast used for secondary fermentation is non-flocculating	Change the yeast for secondary fermentation
Beer is over carbonated in bottle	When opening a bottle of beer, the liquid is forced out with excessive pressure	Added too much priming sugar	Reduce level of sugar addition
		Left too much fermentable sugar after fermentation	Ferment for longer next time
		Bottle has become contaminated by microorganisms, particularly wild yeast	Check cleanliness
Beer has not produced enough carbonation	When you open a bottle of beer, there is no fizz and the beer is flat	Added too little priming sugar	Add more sugar next time
		The beer has not had long enough to produce a secondary fermentation	Leave the beer for longer at a warm temperature to allow the yeast to produce CO_2
		Secondary fermentation at a low temperature	Leave the beer for longer at a warm temperature to allow the yeast to produce CO_2
		Yeast used for secondary fermentation was not viable	Ensure yeast is not dead, check packet

CHAPTER 9

RECIPES

STANDARD PROCEDURE

The following recipes are suggestions for beers to brew based on the topics of Chapters 3 to 6, but, of course, you can choose them at any time. The general procedure is that outlined in Chapter 3, where mash brewing is discussed. However, a step-by-step outline is provided below, which will apply in general to all recipes, although any specific requirements are detailed.

Hot liquor preparation and mashing:

1. Warm your hot liquor tank in plenty of time before you start brewing. Depending on your system, warming up 50ltr might take some time, so a good option is to use a timer that you set the night before. Heat the liquor to a couple of degrees higher than the strike temperature to allow for heat losses. Weigh out the crushed malts and salts in advance so that you are well prepared for the brew.

2. Once you are ready to start brewing, add some hot liquor into the mash tun to cover the filter plate, then leave to stand until it takes the chill away. You can also boil a kettle and add it to the mash tun instead of using the brewing liquor.

3. After a few minutes, the inside of the mash tun should feel warm to the touch. Discard the liquor in the mash tun and proceed to add the mash liquor volume. Measure the temperature and adjust accordingly so that it is as close as possible to the strike temperature. Cooling is easier than heating up the liquor, so it is always best to have a slightly higher temperature in the hot liquor

tank than losing too much heat in the transfer and having to warm up the mash tun with boiling water.

4. Once you are confident that the temperature is stable, add the grist and mix well, ensuring that there are no dry spots. Take the temperature of the mash and adjust if necessary. Remember to start heating up the hot liquor tank to the sparging temperature, 78°C, so that it is ready in time for the sparge.

Sparging:

5. After one hour of letting the mash stand at the target mash temperature, start recirculating until the wort is as clear as possible. Add the wort back carefully to avoid disturbing the bed.

6. Start sparging by adding liquor until a thin layer of hot liquor lies on top of the grain bed, then begin transferring the sweet wort to the kettle. It should take around 30–45 minutes to achieve the full volume in the kettle. It is a good idea to take different samples during the sparge to see how the gravity changes throughout.

Boiling:

7. When you have collected 25ltr in the kettle, give it a good mix and take a sample. At this stage, the gravity should be very close to your target. Add some extra liquor to compensate for the evaporation that will take place during the boil (around 10 per cent, but base this on measurements from a previous brew). While waiting for the wort to get to the boil, weigh out the bittering hops. You can also weigh out the

aroma hops in preparation, but don't mix them with the bittering ones.

8. Before a rolling boil has been reached, add the bittering hops. If you add them shortly before the boil, they will help in controlling it so that it doesn't foam up and overspill.

9. Once you have added the hops and the boil starts, set the timer for 45 minutes. This is when you will be adding copper finings. Check the instructions for the best way to add. If you are using Irish Moss, add it to one cup of hot wort 30 minutes after the boil starts and leave to stand for 15 minutes before adding it to the kettle. If using Protafloc tablets, add directly to the wort 45 minutes into the boil.

10. After 60 minutes, turn off the kettle and add the aroma hops, which will provide aroma and flavour to your beer. The amount of aroma will reflect the recipe, but adjust as you prefer. If you add more than the recipe states, you might need to lower slightly the bittering hops, as you will also get some bitterness from the late aroma additions.

11. Make the final adjustments to the volume and gravity of the wort. This is a critical stage in brewing, as it will dictate how much sugar there is and, in consequence, how much alcohol the yeast can produce.

12. Measure the gravity and volume. Measuring the volume at high temperatures will not be very accurate, as there is an expansion factor with temperature, but at these volumes and for our purposes it is good enough. If the gravity is above the target, you can proceed to liquor back to end up with around 25ltr of wort. If the gravity is low and you have 25ltr wort to adjust, add 70g of sugar per degree of gravity that is missing.

Fermentation and conditioning:

13. Let the wort stand for 10 minutes before cooling down and proceeding to transfer into the fermenter. Remember that once the wort is cooled down, it is the perfect environment for wild yeast and bacteria to grow on, so to avoid ending up with a sour beer, make sure that everything is well cleaned and sanitized for the next steps. Once your wort is at 18°C, add the yeast and close the fermenter. Do not seal the fermenter completely, so as to allow the CO_2 produced during fermentation to escape and avoid any explosions.

14. Leave the fermenter somewhere warm, between 19 and 23°C for ales or 10–13°C for lagers. Monitor the gravity over the next few days. It should finish at between 20 to 25% of the initial gravity depending on the mash temperature. Add the auxiliary finings and chill the beer as cold as possible. After 24 hours of reaching the cooling temperature, take the yeast off the beer if you can and repeat every day or two until ready to bottle. This will help with the clarity of the beer.

15. Condition the beer at this temperature for a minimum of five days for ales and ten days for lagers. Forty-eight hours before you are ready to bottle, add the second set of finings (isinglass, or a vegan-friendly alternative). When you are ready to bottle, transfer the beer from the fermenter to the bright-beer tank. Add 0.1g/ltr of the same yeast you used to ferment, so as to ensure there is enough yeast in the beer for secondary fermentation.

Bottling and kegging:

16. Measure the volume of beer and prepare 2.8g of sugar per litre of beer. Weigh out the sugar and dissolve it in the same amount of boiled water. Make sure that it is completely dissolved and has cooled down before adding it to the bright-beer tank. Ensure that it is properly mixed with the beer.

17. Now you are ready to add the beer to your clean and sanitized bottles or keg. When you have finished bottling, store the bottles or keg somewhere between 16 and 20°C. Let the beer stand for a minimum of a week before opening and trying. If it is not fully carbonated, let the beer stand for a little bit longer. Once carbonated, keep in a cool and dark place.

SUGGESTED LIQUOR FORMULATION FOR 25LTR BREWS

The formulation of salts for addition to your brew is not for the faint-hearted. It involves analysis of your water, linked to an understanding of inorganic chemistry and applying this to your recipe. To help you, we have included a table to use as a guideline. This table will provide a suggestion of what salts to use depending on the type of water you are using. If you find that after brewing these suggestions are not right, you can adjust them gradually to achieve what you want. We have only used calcium salts, as excess calcium has no effect on the beer. Some people use magnesium salts, but this can impart a harsh or metallic bitterness.

The important thing about liquor treatment is that different beer styles require a different quantity of salts. Pale ales have elevated levels of sulphates that enhance the bitterness. Stouts and dark beers need chlorides, as they impart a sweetness to the beer to overcome the coloured malts. It is important to ensure that calcium levels are sufficient to enable both the amylase enzymes and the yeast to work efficiently. The addition of acid or alkalinity (as bicarbonate) to the hot liquor is needed to achieve the correct mash pH to enable the amylase enzymes to work effectively. Bicarbonate is added to counteract the acidic dark malts. For reference, a table is included to show the basis of the calculations.

Reverse osmosis water is where all the salts are removed. Hard water is found when the water is extracted from wells and the water picks up salts as it percolates through the rock strata. Soft water is found when the water comes from reservoirs. Water analysis can often be obtained from your utility company.

Basis of Calculations

Ion	Unit	Reverse Osmosis Water	Soft Water	Hard Water
Alkalinity	mg/l	0	35	300
Chloride	mg/l	0	8	50
Calcium	mg/l	0	22	120
Sulphate	mg/l	0	29	50

Water Treatment Table

Water Treatment	Unit	Reverse Osmosis Water				Soft Water				Hard Water				Where to Add
		Ale	Pale or IPA	Mild Stout Porter	Lager	Ale	Pale or IPA	Mild Stout Porter	Lager	Ale	Pale or IPA	Mild Stout Porter	Lager	
Lactic Acid (80%)	ml	nil	nil	nil	nil	1	nil	nil	nil	25	21	14	25	50ltr of Hot Liquor
Sodium Bicarbonate	g	1.7	5.1	10.2	nil	nil	2.7	7.9	nil	nil	nil	nil	nil	50ltr of Hot Liquor
Calcium Chloride	g	7.9	1.7	11.7	2.9	7.5	11.4	7.9	3.1	5.9	9.8	9.8	3.9	Malt Grist
Calcium Sulphate	g	17.8	6.7	4.5	1.1	16.6	5.4	3.2	nil	15.6	4.5	2.2	nil	Malt Grist

RECIPES FOR CHAPTER 3

The following recipes should give you the basics for some of the traditional styles and ingredients used in brewing, for example tasting and seeing the effects of malts such as crystal or caramalt, the effects on mouthfeel of wheat or oats and how different hops like East Kent Goldings or Simcoe impact flavour.

• •

RECIPE 3.1: 5.1%ABV BITTER

- Target volume = 25ltr
- Bitterness = 35BU
- Colour = 25EBC
- Final gravity = 1.010

Description:

Parameters		Process Parameters	
ABV (%)	5.1	Strike temperature	76°C
OG	1.049	Mash temperature	69°C
PG	1.010	Liquor to grist ratio	2.7
Bitterness (BU)	35	Liquor volume (ltr)	14
Colour (EBC)	25	Mash time (hours)	1
Mash efficiency (%)	80	Boil time (hours)	1
Hop effiiency (%)	35		
Volume (ltr)	25		
CO_2 (g/ltr)	3.5		

Ingredients:

	Specification	Amount
Water Treatment		Refer to water
Alkalinity	Adjust in HLB	treatment
Calcium sulphate	Add to mash	table for
Calcium chloride		pale ale
Cereals and Adjuncts		
Pale malt	4EBC	4.3kg
Crystal malt	100–130EBC	280g
Amber malt	50EBC	280g

Hops

Bittering: Target (leaf)	10% α acids	25g
East Kent Goldings (leaf)		50g
Challenger (leaf)		50g

Yeast

British ale yeast	11–25g

Ancillary Materials

Add at end of boil:	Irish Moss or	1tsp
	Protafloc tablet	¼
Add at end of fermentation:	Auxiliary finings	90g
	Isinglass finings	90ml
	Priming sugar	3.2g
	per 500ml bottle	

• •

RECIPE 3.2: 4.0%ABV BLONDE

- Target volume = 25ltr
- Bitterness = 25BU
- Colour = 6EBC
- Final gravity = 1.006

Description:

Parameters		Process Parameters	
ABV (%)	4.0	Strike temperature	72°C
OG	1.037	Mash temperature	65°C
PG	1.006	Liquor to grist ratio	2.7
Bitterness (BU)	25	Liquor volume (ltr)	10.5
Colour (EBC)	6	Mash time (hours)	1
Mash efficiency (%)	80	Boil time (hours)	1
Hop efficiency (%)	35		
Volume (ltr)	25		
CO_2 (g/ltr)	4		

Ingredients:

	Specification	Amount
Water Treatment		Refer to water
Alkalinity	Adjust in HLB	treatment
Calcium sulphate	Add to mash	table for
Calcium chloride		pale ale
Cereals and Adjuncts		
Pale malt	4EBC	1.85kg
Lager malt	3.5	1.85kg
Torrified wheat	3.5EBC	160g
Hops		
Bittering: Target (leaf)	10% α acids	20g
East Kent Goldings (leaf)		80g
Yeast		
British ale yeast		11–25g
Ancillary Materials		
Add 45 minutes	Irish Moss or	1tsp
into the boil:	Protafloc tablet	¼
Add at end of	Auxiliary finings	90g
fermentation:	Isinglass finings	90ml
	Priming sugar	3.2g
	per 500ml bottle	

• •

RECIPE 3.3: 4.2%ABV GOLDEN ALE

- Target volume = 25ltr
- Bitterness = 35BU
- Colour = 8EBC
- Final gravity = 1.006

Description:

Parameters		Process Parameters	
ABV (%)	4.2	Strike temperature	72°C
OG	1.038	Mash temperature	65°C
PG	1.006	Liquor to grist ratio	2.7
Bitterness (BU)	35	Liquor volume (ltr)	11
Colour (EBC)	8	Mash time (hours)	1
Mash efficiency (%)	80	Boil time (hours)	1
Hop efficiency (%)	35		
Volume (ltr)	25		
CO_2 (g/ltr)	4		

Ingredients:

	Specification	Amount
Water Treatment		Refer to
Alkalinity	Adjust in HLB	water
Calcium sulphate	Add to mash	treatment
Calcium chloride		table for
		pale ale
Cereals and Adjuncts		
Pale malt	4EBC	2kg
Lager malt	3.5	1.6kg
Caragold	14EBC	430g
Hops		
Bittering: Target (leaf)	10% α acids	25g
Willamette (leaf)		30g
First Gold (leaf)		70g
Yeast		
British ale yeast		11–25g
Ancillary Materials		
Add 45 minutes	Irish Moss or	1tsp
into the boil:	Protafloc tablet	¼
Add at end of	Auxiliary finings	90g
fermentation :	Isinglass finings	90ml
	Priming sugar	3.2g
	per 500ml bottle	

RECIPE 3.4: 4.0%ABV PALE ALE

* Target volume 25ltr
* Bitterness = 30BU
* Colour = 13EBC
* Final gravity = 1.008

Description:

Parameters		Process Parameters	
ABV (%)	4.0	Strike temperature	74°C
OG	1.039	Mash temperature	67°C
PG	1.008	Liquor to grist ratio	2.7
Bitterness (BU)	30	Liquor volume (ltr)	11
Colour (EBC)	13	Mash time (hours)	1
Mash efficiency (%)	80	Boil time (hours)	1
Hop efficiency (%)	35		
Volume (ltr)	25		
CO_2 (g/ltr)	4		

Ingredients:

	Specification	Amount
Water Treatment		Refer to water
Alkalinity	Adjust in HLB	treatment
Calcium sulphate	Add to mash	table for
Calcium chloride		pale ale
Cereals and Adjuncts		
Pale malt	4EBC	3.4kg
Caramalt	24EBC	600g
Torrified Wheat	3.5EBC	200g
Hops		
Bittering: Magnum (leaf)	10% α acids	20g
Simcoe (leaf)		75g
Amarillo (leaf)		75g
Yeast		
American ale yeast		11–25g

Ancillary Materials

Add 45 minutes into the boil:	Irish Moss or	1tsp
	Protafloc tablet	¼
Add at end of fermentation:	Auxiliary finings	90g
	Isinglass finings	90ml
	Priming sugar per 500ml bottle	3.3g

RECIPE 3.5: 4.3%ABV PALE ALE

* Target volume = 25ltr
* Bitterness = 25BU
* Colour = 8EBC
* Final gravity = 1.008

Description:

Parameters		Process Parameters	
ABV (%)	4.3	Strike temperature	76°C
OG	1.042	Mash temperature	69°C
PG	1.008	Liquor to grist ratio	2.7
Bitterness (BU)	25	Liquor volume (ltr)	12
Colour (EBC)	8	Mash time (hours)	1
Mash efficiency (%)	80	Boil time (hours)	1
Hop efficiency (%)	35		
Volume (ltr)	25		
CO_2 (g/ltr)	4		

Ingredients:

	Specification	Amount
Water Treatment		Refer to water
Alkalinity	Adjust in HLB	treatment
Calcium sulphate	Add to mash	table for
Calcium chloride		pale ale

Cereals and Adjuncts

Pale malt	4EBC	3.5kg
Wheat malt	3EBC	650g
Golden naked oats	15EBC	240g

Hops

Bittering: Challenger (leaf) 8% α acids	22g
Challenger (leaf)	65g
Cascade (leaf)	65g

Yeast

American ale yeast	11–25g

Ancillary Materials

Add 45 minutes into the boil:	Irish Moss or Protafloc tablet	1tsp ¼
Add at end of fermentation:	Auxiliary finings	90g
	Isinglass finings	90ml
	Priming sugar per 500ml bottle	3.4g

RECIPES FOR CHAPTER 4

When choosing the ingredients for a brew, the effects on the final product can vary substantially, depending on quantities or the time of addition. When it comes to malts, these can be subtle, or more profound flavour and colour differences due to problems with extracts or low run-offs during sparging. The recipes in Chapter 4 explore different malts and the effects on the final product.

The Imperial Stout consists of a range of darker malts that will contribute heavily to the final character of the beer and at 9.4%ABV it is not for the faint-hearted. When brewing higher ABV beers you might struggle with fitting all the grist in the mash tun, so make sure that your starch conversion vessel is big enough before you start brewing. But you could also brew a second, lower ABV, beer from the sugars that are left behind in the mash. Check the gravity of the wort left in the mash tun. You will probably be able to continue sparging, collecting in a second kettle to brew another 25ltr.

Pilsner malt instead of pale malt, which will be slightly lighter in colour and grainier in character, is used in lagers. The proposed recipe also has an adjunct used in many commercial lagers, torrefied maize, which will add a corn character to the beer. Mashing in at a lower temperature will also help with getting the light mouthfeel typical of this style.

Red ale number one uses roasted barley to produce a red hue, the same roasted barley that is used for producing the pitch-black colour of a dry stout. When brewing this beer, you could add the roasted barley along with all the other malts into the mash, but if you would prefer to take away a bit of the harshness that this adjunct will give the beer, sprinkle it on top of the grain bed when you've finished the mash and are ready to start sparging (but don't forget about it!).

The second red ale recipe uses rye malt and Munich to add red colour to the beer rather than roasted barley. It also has a bit more hop character, which might deviate from the original style but should complement the maltiness of this beer. This recipe also includes rice hulls, which will not impart taste or colour but will help with filtration during sparging. Some malts and adjuncts are high in beta-glucans, which, if they are found in high proportion in the mash, can cause problems with filtration, leading to the risk of a stuck mash. Adding the rice hulls will help to prevent this in this case, as you will be using rye malt as one of the main malts.

Finally, there are two stout recipes that should provide you with a nice rich dark beer, but with different characters each. The first one will be more in style with a dry stout, with a harsher coffee taste coming from the roasted barley (which is actually not a malt, as the barley has not gone through the malting process). The second recipe has roasted barley too, but should have a much maltier taste along the coffee notes from the roasted barley and black malt. If you prefer smoother stouts, you can substitute the roasted barley for Carafa III and in the second recipe you could exchange both the roasted barley and the black malt for this one.

RECIPE 4.1: 9.4%ABV IMPERIAL STOUT

- Target volume = 25ltr
- Bitterness = 50BU
- Colour = 670EBC
- Final gravity = 1.018

Description:

Parameters		Process Parameters	
ABV (%)	9.4	Strike temperature	72°C
OG	1.090	Mash temperature	65°C
PG	1.018	Liquor to grist ratio	2.7
Bitterness (BU)	50	Liquor volume (ltr)	30
Colour (EBC)	670	Mash time (hours)	1
Mash efficiency (%)	70	Boil time (hours)	1
Hop efficiency (%)	35		
Volume (ltr)	25		
CO_2 (g/ltr)	4		

Ingredients:

	Specification	Amount
Water Treatment		Refer to
Alkalinity	Adjust in HLB	water
Calcium sulphate	Add to mash	treatment
Calcium chloride		for stout
Cereals and Adjuncts		
Pale malt	4EBC	7.6kg
Roasted barley	1300EBC	620g
Chocolate malt	900EBC	620g
Brown malt	400EBC	620g
Aromatic malt	60EBC	560g
Flaked barley	1EBC	1kg
Hops		
Bittering: Bramling Cross (leaf)	6% α acids	60g
Bramling Cross (leaf)		75g
Fuggles (leaf)		50g

Yeast

British ale yeast	20–30g

Ancillary Materials

Add 45 minutes into the boil:	Irish Moss or Protafloc tablet	1tsp ¼
Add at end of fermentation:	Auxiliary finings	90g
	Isinglass finings	90ml
	Priming sugar per 500ml bottle	3.4g

RECIPE 4.2: 4.8%ABV LAGER

- Target volume = 25ltr
- Bitterness = 14BU
- Colour = 7EBC
- Final gravity = 1.005

Description:

Parameters		Process Parameters	
ABV (%)	4.8	Strike temperature	70°C
OG	1.042	Mash temperature	63°C
PG	1.005	Liquor to grist ratio	2.7
Bitterness (BU)	14	Liquor volume (ltr)	12.2
Colour (EBC)	7	Mash time (hours)	1
Mash efficiency (%)	80	Boil time (hours)	1
Hop efficiency (%)	35		
Volume (ltr)	25		
CO_2 (g/ltr)	4.5		

Ingredients:

	Specification	Amount
Water Treatment		Refer to
Alkalinity	Adjust in HLB	water
Calcium sulphate	Add to mash	treatment
Calcium chloride		for lager
Cereals and Adjuncts		
Lager malt	3.5EBC	2.5kg
Vienna malt	7EBC	1.43kg
Torrefied maize	0.5EBC	340g
Torrefied wheat	3.5EBC	230g
Hops		
Bittering: Magnum (leaf)	11% α acids	6.4g
First Gold (leaf)		50g
Yeast		
Lager yeast		11–25g
Ancillary Materials		
Add 45 minutes into the boil :	Irish Moss or Protafloc tablet	1tsp ¼
Add at end of fermentation:	Auxiliary finings	90g
	Isinglass finings	90ml
	Priming sugar per 500ml bottle	4.4g

• •

RECIPE 4.3: 4.5%ABV RED ALE

- Target volume = 25ltr
- Bitterness = 28BU
- Colour = 32EBC
- Final gravity = 1.010

Description: Parameters		**Process Parameters**	
ABV (%)	4.5	Strike temperature	72°C
OG	1.045	Mash temperature	65°C
PG	1.010	Liquor to grist ratio	2.7
Bitterness (BU)	28	Liquor volume (ltr)	13
Colour (EBC)	32	Mash time (hours)	1
Mash efficiency (%)	80	Boil time (hours)	1
Hop efficiency (%)	35		
Volume (ltr)	25		
CO_2 (g/ltr)	4		

Ingredients:

	Specification	Amount
Water Treatment		Refer to
Alkalinity	Adjust in HLB	water
Calcium sulphate	Add to mash	treatment
Calcium chloride		table for
		pale ale
Cereals and Adjuncts		
Pale malt	4EBC	3.9kg
Caramalt	24EBC	520g
Roasted barley	1300EBC	40g
Torrefied wheat	3.5EBC	370g
Hops		
Bittering: First Gold (leaf)	7.5% α acids	27g
First Gold (leaf)		38g
East Kent Goldings (leaf)		12g
Yeast		
British ale yeast		11–25g
Ancillary Materials		
Add 45 minute into the boil:	Irish Moss or Protafloc tablet	1tsp ¼

Add at end of fermentation:	Auxillary finings		90g
	Isinglass finings		90ml
	Priming sugar		3.8g
	per 500ml bottle		

Crystal malt		150EBC	170g
Rice hulls		NA	110g

Hops

Bittering: Challenger (leaf)	8% α acids	24g
Challenger (leaf)		40g
Cascade (Leaf)		60g

Yeast

British ale yeast	11–25g

Ancillary Materials

Add 45 minutes into the boil:	Irish Moss or	1tsp
	Protafloc tablet	¼
Add at end of fermentation:	Auxiliary finings	90g
	Isinglass finings	90ml
	Priming sugar	3.8g
	per 500ml bottle	

RECIPE 4.4: 5.2%ABV RED ALE

- Target volume = 25ltr
- Bitterness = 27BU
- Colour = 36EBC
- Final gravity = 1.012

Description:

Parameters		Process Parameters	
ABV (%)	5.2	Strike temperature	72°C
OG	1.052	Mash temperature	65°C
PG	1.012	Liquor to grist ratio	2.7
Bitterness (BU)	27	Liquor volume (ltr)	13.7
Colour (EBC)	36	Mash time (hours)	1
Mash efficiency (%)	80	Boil time (hours)	1
Hop efficiency (%)	35		
Volume (ltr)	25		
CO_2 (g/ltr)	4		

Ingredients:

	Specification	Amount
Water Treatment		Refer to
Alkalinity	Adjust in HLB	water
Calcium sulphate	Add to mash	treatment
Calcium chloride		table for
		pale ale
Cereals and Adjuncts		
Pale malt	4EBC	2.4kg
Munich	20EBC	1.53kg
Wheat malt	3EBC	760g
Rye malt	32EBC	570g

RECIPE 4.5: 4.5%ABV STOUT

- Target volume = 25ltr
- Bitterness = 30BU
- Colour = 290EBC
- Final gravity = 1.009

Description:

Parameters		Process Parameters	
ABV (%)	4.5	Strike temperature	74°C
OG	1044	Mash temperature	67°C
PG	1.009	Liquor to grist ratio	2.7
Bitterness (BU)	30	Liquor volume (ltr)	11.5
Colour (EBC)	290	Mash time (hours)	1
Mash efficiency (%)	80	Boil time (hours)	1
Hop efficiency (%)	35		
Volume (ltr)	25		
CO_2 (g/ltr)	3.5		

Ingredients:

	Specification	Amount
Water Treatment		Refer to
Alkalinity	Adjust in HLB	water
Calcium sulphate	Add to mash	treatment
Calcium chloride		table for
		stout
Cereals and Adjuncts		
Pale malt	4EBC	3.6kg
Roasted barely	1300EBC	520g
Flaked barley	1EBC	440g
Hops		
Bittering: Bramling Cross (leaf) 6% α acids		36g
Bramling Cross (leaf)		50g
Yeast		
British ale yeast		11–25g
Ancillary Materials		
Add 45 minutes	Irish Moss or	1tsp
into the boil:	Protafloc tablet	¼
Add at end of	Auxiliary finings	90g
fermentation:	Isinglass finings	90ml
	Priming sugar	3.4g
	per 500ml bottle	

● ●

RECIPE 4.6: 6%ABV STOUT

- Target volume = 25ltr
- Bitterness = 21BU
- Colour = 218EBC
- Final gravity = 1.012

Description:

Parameters		Process Parameters	
ABV (%)	6	Strike temperature	72°C
OG	1.058	Mash temperature	65°C
PG	1.012	Liquor to grist ratio	2.7
Bitterness (BU)	21	Liquor volume (ltr)	15.5
Colour (EBC)	218	Mash time (hours)	1
Mash efficiency (%)	80	Boil time (hours)	1
Hop efficiency (%)	35		
Volume (ltr)	25		
CO_2 (g/ltr)	3.5		

Ingredients:

	Specification	Amount
Water Treatment		Refer to
Alkalinity	Adjust in HLB	water
Calcium sulphate	Add to mash	treatment
Calcium chloride		table for
		stout
Cereals and Adjuncts		
Pale malt	4EBC	4.6kg
Crystal malt	150EBC	600g
Brown malt	400EBC	320g
Black malt	1300EBC	200g
Roasted barley	1300EBC	60g
Hops		
Bittering: Fuggles (leaf)	4% α acids	38g
Fuggles (leaf)		38g
Goldings (leaf)		38g
Yeast		
British ale yeast		11–25g
Ancillary Materials		
Add 45 minutes	Irish Moss or	1tsp
into the boil:	Protafloc tablet	¼

Add at end of fermentation:	Auxillary finings	90g
	Isinglass finings	90ml
	Priming sugar	3.4g
	per 500ml bottle	

RECIPES FOR CHAPTER 5

Chapter 5 explores the world of hops. This is an extensive area, with new hops coming into play every year and different techniques to try so as to get the best hop character. The following recipes are a first approach to this very popular ingredient.

With the lager recipe you can explore the family of the noble hops. There are two options in the recipe, but feel free to combine them or swap them for other noble hops and detect the subtle differences.

The West Coast IPA should have quite a good hop character along with a decent amount of bitterness, with the malts relegated to a second place but still important to provide a good balance and mouthfeel to the final product. And the IPA will have a good hop character, thanks to two very popular hops, Simcoe and Citra. Although a bit less potent than the West Coast, it should still be a hop-forward beer.

For both styles of IPA, once cool, add the yeast. Monitor the fermentation and when it is getting towards the end, round about 1.014–1.016 gravity, add the pellet hops. The pellet hops can be added straight into the beer, but, depending on your system, it might take quite a long time for them to drop to the bottom, or you might be taking bits of hops with the beer into the bottle when the time comes. If you don't want to risk this, or have to wait around for the beer to drop bright, sanitize a muslin bag, add the hops and drop it in the fermenter. Leave for 24 hours before you start cooling the beer to conditioning temperature. Condition for one week before you bottle it.

Different brewers like adding the hops at different stages. In these recipes, the recommendation is to add the hops just before the end of fermentation. Alternatively, you could try adding them after cooling the beer down to conditioning temperature and see how that affects the flavour profile.

Likewise, with the hops added during the boil, you could split the additions at different stages, but remember that the longer the time in boiling wort, the more volatiles will be lost and the more α acids will be converted into bittering iso-α acids. If you decide to split them, you might want to reduce the bittering hops slightly. You could also reduce the temperature of the wort before adding the final set of hops to the boil. If you keep it to just under 80°C, there should be less conversion of the α acids into the iso-α acids form.

Much less hop-forward than the West Coast IPA, the strong bitter recipe will provide you with a nice copper-coloured beer with a decent level of maltiness coming from the crystal malt and balanced with the aroma and flavours of some traditional hops like East Kent Goldings and First Gold, plus a decent bitterness to cut through the maltiness. These hops won't be as powerful as the ones used in the West Coast or the IPA, but they should still come through in the beer.

• •

RECIPE 5.1: 4.3%ABV LAGER

- Target volume = 25ltr
- Bitterness = 8BU
- Colour = 7.5EBC
- Final gravity = 1.003

Description:

Parameters		Process Parameters	
ABV (%)	4.3	Strike temperature	70°C
OG	1.036	Mash temperature	63°C
PG	1.003	Liquor to grist ratio	2.7
Bitterness (BU)	8	Liquor volume (ltr)	9
Colour (EBC)	7.5	Mash time (hours)	1
Mash efficiency (%)	80	Boil time (hours)	1
Hop efficiency (%)	35		
Volume (ltr)	25		
CO_2 (g/ltr)	4.5		

Ingredients:

	Specification	Amount
Water Treatment		Refer to
Alkalinity	Adjust in HLB	water
Calcium sulphate	Add to mash	treatment
Calcium chloride		table for
		lager
Cereals and Adjuncts		
Lager malt	3.5EBC	2.5kg
Caramalt	24EBC	350g
Torrified wheat	3.5EBC	220g
Sugar	0EBC	370g
Hops		
Bittering: Tettnanger (leaf) 5% α acids		11g
Saaz or Hallertau Mittelfüh (leaf)		50g
Yeast		
Lager yeast		11–25g
Ancillary Materials		
Add 45 minutes	Irish Moss or	1tsp
into the boil	Protafloc tablet	¼
Add at end of	Auxiliary finings	90g
fermentation	Isinglass finings	90ml
	Priming sugar	4.6g
	per 500ml bottle	

● ●

RECIPE 5.2: 6.7%ABV WEST COAST IPA

- Target volume = 25ltr
- Bitterness = 45BU
- Colour = 18EBC
- Final gravity = 1.013

Description:

Parameters		Process Parameters	
ABV (%)	6.7	Strike temperature	72°C
OG	1.065	Mash temperature	65°C
PG	1.013	Liquor to grist ratio	2.7
Bitterness (BU)	45	Liquor volume (ltr)	19
Colour (EBC)	18	Mash time (hours)	1
Mash efficiency (%)	80	Boil time (hours)	1
Hop efficiency (%)	35		
Volume (ltr)	25		
CO_2 (g/ltr)	5		

Ingredients:

	Specification	Amount
Water Treatment		Refer to
Alkalinity	Adjust in HLB	water
Calcium sulphate	Add to mash	treatment
Calcium chloride		table for IPA
Cereals and Adjuncts		
Pale malt	4EBC	5.8kg
Dextrin malt	2.5EBC	680g
Golden naked oats	15EBC	370g
Hops		
Bittering: Centenial (leaf) 10% α acids		27g
Mosaic (Leaf)		38g
Mandarina Bavaria (leaf)		38g
Centennial (leaf)		38g
Amarillo (leaf)		38g
Mosaic (pellet)		25g
Mandarina Bavaria (pellet)		25g
Centennial (pellet)		25g
Amarillo (pellet)		25g
Yeast		
American ale yeast		20–30g
Ancillary Materials		
Add 45 minutes	Irish Moss or	1tsp
into the boil:	Protafloc tablet	¼

Add at end of	Auxiliary finings	90g
fermentation:	Isinglass finings	90ml
	Priming sugar	4.8g
	per 500ml bottle	

Hops

Bittering: Magnum (leaf)	10% α acids	25g
Simcoe (leaf)		50g
Citra (leaf)		50g
Simcoe (pellets)		25g
Citra (pellets)		25g

Yeast

British ale yeast	11–25g

Ancillary Materials

Add 45 minutes	Irish Moss or	1tsp
into the boil:	Protafloc tablet	¼
Add at end of	Auxiliary finings	90g
fermentation:	Isinglass finings	90ml
	Priming sugar	4.4g
	per 500ml bottle	

RECIPE 5.3: 5.5%ABV IPA

- Target volume = 25ltr
- Bitterness = 35BU
- Colour = 18EBC
- Final gravity = 1.012

Description:

Parameters		Process Parameters	
ABV (%)	5.5	Strike temperature	75°C
OG	1.055	Mash temperature	68°C
PG	1.012	Liquor to grist ratio	2.7
Bitterness (BU)	35	Liquor volume (ltr)	15.5
Colour (EBC)	18	Mash time (hours)	1
Mash efficiency (%)	80	Boil time (hours)	1
Hop efficiency (%)	35		
Volume (ltr)	25		
CO_2 (g/ltr)	4.5		

Ingredients:

	Specification	Amount
Water Treatment	Adjust in HLB	Refer to
Alkalinity	Add to mash	water
Calcium sulphate		treatment
Calcium chloride		for IPA
Cereals and Adjuncts		
Pale malt	4EBC	4.6kg
Caramalt	24EBC	930g
Torrified wheat	3.5EBC	310g

RECIPE 5.4: 5.0%ABV ESB

- Target volume = 25ltr
- Bitterness = 35BU
- Colour = 30EBC
- Final gravity = 1.010

Description:

Parameters		Process Parameters	
ABV (%)	5.0	Strike temperature	72°C
OG	1.048	Mash temperature	65°C
PG	1.010	Liquor to grist ratio	2.7
Bitterness (BU)	35	Liquor volume (ltr)	13.7
Colour (EBC)	30	Mash time (hours)	1
Mash efficiency (%)	80	Boil time (hours)	1
Hop efficiency (%)	35		
Volume (ltr)	25		
CO_2 (g/ltr)	4		

Ingredients:

	Specification	Amount
Water Treatment		Refer to
Alkalinity	Adjust in HLB	water
Calcium sulphate	Add to mash	treatment
Calcium chloride		for IPA
Cereals and Adjuncts		
Pale malt	4EBC	4.3kg
Crystal malt	100EBC	540g
Torrefied wheat	3.5EBC	270g
Hops		
Bittering: Target (leaf)	10% α acids	25g
First Gold (leaf)		65g
East Kent Goldings (leaf)		65g
Yeast		
British ale yeast		11–25g
Ancillary Materials		
Add 45 minutes	Irish Moss or	1tsp
into the boil:	Protafloc tablet	¼
Add at end of	Auxiliary finings	90g
fermentation :	Isinglass finings	90ml
	Priming sugar	3.8g
	per 500ml bottle	

RECIPES FOR CHAPTER 6

Another amazing world to explore comes at a much smaller scale than hops, one that we can only see through a microscope, but with these recipes we should definitely be able to taste the difference. The four recipes that follow should give you an insight into what effects yeast has on the final character of the beer.

Saison beers tend to have a fruity, spicy character, which is given to them by the strain of yeast, so it is essential to use a Saison yeast when brewing this beer. These types of yeast also tend to be highly attenuating,

so expect the beer to have a dry finish. Make sure the beer has finished fermenting before bottling, so that you don't end up with exploding bottles rather than a nice drink.

When brewing the Trappist beer, the yeasts used for this style of beer tend to add quite a lot of phenolic compounds as well as esters. These give the beer a complex flavour, with the spicy and fruity characters coming through. Try to control the fermentation temperature as best as you can and especially do not let them ferment at high temperatures, as this might lead to elevated levels of higher (fusel) alcohol and a taste that you don't want in the beer. As it is a high ABV beer, remember that you can do the same as with the Imperial Stout and brew a second beer from the same mash.

There are also two examples of wheat beers, a light-coloured one and a dark wheat beer (Dunkel Weissbier). These styles of beer also use different strains of yeast – some will produce a more subtle character than others, or will be producing more phenols than esters, or vice versa. Fermentation temperature will also play a part – try to prevent it from rising too high so that the beer does not become unbalanced, with off flavours. If you want to give your beer a bit of a twist, add crushed coriander seeds to the boil and some fresh orange or lemon peel too.

The first recipe for wheat beer could also be the base for a Berliner Weisse style beer. For this, substitute the yeast for already prepared culture blends that will provide the sourness traditional of this style, or experiment by adding cultures of lactobacillus, thus entering the world of bacteria.

Note: do not add Auxiliary or Isinglass to the wheat beers to keep them hazy.

RECIPE 6.1: 5.8%ABV SAISON

- Target volume = 25ltr
- Bitterness = 25BU
- Colour = 14.5EBC
- Final gravity = 1.008

Description:
ParametersProcess Parameters

ABV (%)	5.6	Strike temperature	72°C
OG	1.051	Mash temperature	65°C
PG	1.008	Liquor to grist ratio	2.7
Bitterness (BU)	25	Liquor volume (ltr)	14.4
Colour (EBC)	14.5	Mash time (hours)	1
Mash efficiency (%)	80	Boil time (hours)	1
Hop efficiency (%)	35		
Volume (ltr)	25		
CO_2 (g/ltr)	5		

Ingredients:

	Specification	Amount
Water Treatment		Refer to
Alkalinity	Adjust in HLB	water
Calcium sulphate	Add to mash	treatment
Calcium chloride		for ale
Cereals and Adjuncts		
Vienna malt	7EBC	3.44kg
Rye malt	12EBC	720g
Wheat malt	3EBC	1.06 kg
Rice hulls	NA	130g
Hops		
Bittering: Northern Brewer (leaf) 7.5% α acids		23g
Styrian Bobek (leaf)		53g
Centennial (leaf)		23g
Yeast		
Saison yeast		11–25g

Ancillary Materials

Add 45 minutes	Irish Moss or	1tsp
into the boil:	Protafloc tablet	¼
Add at end of	Auxiliary finings	90g
fermentation:	Isinglass finings	90ml
	Priming sugar	3.8g
	per 500ml bottle	

RECIPE 6.2: 7.5%ABV TRAPPIST

- Target volume = 25ltr
- Bitterness = 35BU
- Colour = 53EBC
- Final gravity = 1.016

Description:
ParametersProcess Parameters

ABV (%)	7.5	Strike temperature	72°C
OG	1.075	Mash temperature	65°C
PG	1.016	Liquor to grist ratio	2.7
Bitterness (BU)	35	Liquor volume (ltr)	21
Colour (EBC)	53	Mash time (hours)	1
Mash efficiency (%)	70	Boil time (hours)	1
Hop efficiency (%)	35		
Volume (ltr)	25		
CO_2 (g/ltr)	4.5		

Ingredients:

	Specification	Amount
Water Treatment		Refer to
Alkalinity	Adjust in HLB	water
Calcium sulphate	Add to mash	treatment
Calcium chloride		for ale
Cereals and Adjuncts		
Pale malt	4EBC	7.1kg
Crystal malt	150EBC	480g
Aromatic malt	60EBC	460g
Torrefied wheat	3EBC	930g
Hops		
Bittering: Magnum (leaf)	10% α acids	25g
Saaz (leaf)		50g
Yeast		
Trappist yeast		20–30g

Ancillary Materials

Add 45 minutes into the boil:	Irish Moss or Protafloc tablet	1tsp ¼
Add at end of fermentation:	Auxiliary finings	90g
	Isinglass finings	90ml
	Priming sugar per 500ml bottle	4.4g

- -

RECIPE 6.3: 5%ABV WHEAT BEER

- Target volume = 25ltr
- Bitterness = 12BU
- Colour = 8EBC
- Final gravity = 1.011

Description:

Parameters		Process Parameters	
ABV (%)	5	Strike temperature	72°C
OG	1.050	Mash temperature	65°C
PG	1.011	Liquor to grist ratio	2.7
Bitterness (BU)	12	Liquor volume (ltr)	14
Colour (EBC)	8	Mash time (hours)	1
Mash efficiency (%)	80	Boil time (hours)	1
Hop efficiency (%)	35		
Volume (ltr)	25		
CO_2 (g/ltr)	5.5		

Ingredients:

	Specification	Amount
Water Treatment		Refer to
Alkalinity	Adjust in HLB	water
Calcium sulphate	Add to mash	treatment
Calcium chloride		for lager

Cereals and Adjuncts

Pale malt	4EBC	2.6kg
Wheat malt	2.5EBC	2.6kg

Hops

Bittering: Magnum (leaf)	10% α acids	7.5g
Northern Brewer (Leaf)		25g

Yeast

Wheat beer yeast		11–25g

Ancillary Materials

Add 45 minutes into the boil:	Irish Moss or Protafloc tablet	1tsp ¼
Add at end of fermentation:	Priming sugar per 500ml bottle	5.3g

Optional Additions

Add 45 minutes into the boil:	Crushed coriander seed	50g
Add 50 minutes into the boil:	Fresh orange/ lemon peel	75g

- -

RECIPE 6.4: 5.3%ABV DUNKEL WEISSBIER

- Target volume = 25ltr
- Bitterness = 16BU
- Colour = 36EBC
- Final gravity = 1.012

Description:

Parameters		Process Parameters	
ABV (%)	5.3	Strike temperature	72°C
OG	1.052	Mash temperature	65°C
PG	1.012	Liquor to grist ratio	2.7
Bitterness (BU)	16	Liquor volume (ltr)	15
Colour (EBC)	36	Mash time (hours)	1
Mash efficiency (%)	80	Boil time (hours)	1
Hop efficiency (%)	35		
Volume (ltr)	25		
CO_2 (g/ltr)	5.5		

Ingredients:

	Specification	Amount
Water Treatment		Refer
Alkalinity	Adjust in HLB	to water
Calcium sulphate	Add to mash	treatment
Calcium chloride		for lager
Cereals and Adjuncts		
Wheat malt	2.5EBC	3.6kg
Munich malt	20EBC	1.74kg
Crystal Dark	250EBC	180g
Hops		
Bittering: Northern Brewer (Leaf)	9.5% α acids	12g
Northern Brewer (Leaf)		35g
Yeast		
Wheat beer yeast		11–25g

Ancillary Materials		
Add 45 minutes into the boil:	Irish Moss or	1tsp
	Protafloc tablet	¼
	Priming sugar per 500ml bottle	5.3g

RECIPES FOR CHAPTER 7

These last recipes are an introduction to adding other ingredients to your brews to make them a bit different. You can also take some of the other recipes as a base and add fruits, herbs, spices or different yeasts and bacteria, but any other effects that these ingredients might have on the beer may need to be taken into account. If adding puree or juice, the sugar content is likely to be increased and in turn the ABV of the final product.

In the case of the Mango IPA, for example, the recipe is calculated based on a puree of around 23 Brix. A higher or lower content of sugar in the puree could lead to more or less alcohol. The mango puree can be added at different stages to protect the flavour, but the suggestion is to add it during fermentation. Let the yeast begin working and get a good head start before adding the mango puree, but do so before the fermentation stops. It will add extra sugar to the beer, so fermentation will go on for a bit longer.

When making the Raspberry Sour, there are different ways of souring a beer, so make sure that you have decided how to achieve this before commencing brewing. The easiest way is by adding a mixed culture to the cold wort at around 20°C. These mixed cultures may have different strains of yeast and bacteria, which will provide both alcohol and lactic acid. This method might take a bit longer to sour your beer depending on the strains you use.

If deciding on a kettle sour, make sure that you can hold the temperature in the kettle at around 30°C for 24–48 hours. This technique will be more complicated and risky than the previous one, but will give you a sour beer much faster. After boiling for an hour with the hops, bring the boiling wort inside the kettle down to the required temperature. Different cultures may have optimal temperatures, so check this before proceeding. Once you have achieved the right temperature, add the souring culture and leave for 24–48 hours. Try the wort during this time to see how the souring process is going and stop it on reaching a level you are happy with.

It is recommended to acidify the wort before

adding the culture. This will prevent some spoilage bacteria from growing. Add lactic acid bit by bit to the wort while measuring the pH with a meter; ideally, you should get the pH somewhere in the region of 4.0–4.3.

Once you are happy with the sourness of the beer, reboil the beer for 10–15 minutes to kill the bacteria, cool down and ferment as normal with a brewing yeast strain.

The raspberries can be added in the fermenter or in the boil. It is safer to add them during the boil to minimize the risk of contamination. Add them to the second boil, 10 minutes before the end. If you decide to add them to the fermenter, it is best to freeze the raspberries first, then defrost them and add them while the beer is fermenting. Depending on how the raspberries are added, they will add more or less sugar to the wort; you could expect an increase in gravity and around 0.15% increase in ABV.

Honey can be used as a priming sugar, or be added during the boil or fermentation, contributing to the total alcohol level of the beer. In the Honey Beer recipe, it is contributing around 7% of the total sugars that the yeast will use to produce alcohol. You can choose to add it at the end of the boil or during fermentation. If added during the boil, there will probably be a slight loss of flavour, but it will be easier to mix and dissolve in the wort. Adding it during fermentation will preserve some of the more volatile compounds, but the honey must be runny and you might want to consider dissolving it in a similar amount of boiling water before adding it to the fermenter. Boil the water and let it cool down a bit before adding the honey to preserve the flavours. Dissolve the honey, let it cool down a little further, then add to the fermenter. You can add it at the start or halfway through fermentation. Once the beer has fully fermented, proceed as usual.

RECIPE 7.1: 5.2%ABV MANGO IPA

- Target volume = 25ltr
- Bitterness = 25BU
- Colour = 14EBC
- Final gravity = 1.010

Description:

Parameters		Process Parameters	
ABV (%)	5.2	Strike temperature	72°C
OG	1.050	Mash temperature	65°C
PG	1.010	Liquor to grist ratio	2.7
Bitterness (BU)	25	Liquor volume (ltr)	14
Colour (EBC)	14	Mash time (hours)	1
Mash efficiency (%)	80	Boil time (hours)	1
Hop efficiency (%)	35		
Volume (ltr)	25		
CO_2 (g/ltr)	5.5		

Ingredients:

	Specification	Amount
Water Treatment		
Alkalinity	Adjust in HLB	Refer to water
Calcium sulphate	Add to mash	treatment
Calcium chloride		table for IPA
Cereals and Adjuncts		
Pale malt	4EBC	3.7kg
Caragold	15EBC	850g
Golden Naked Oats	15EBC	290g
Torrefied wheat	3EBC	290g
Hops		
Bittering: Magnum 10% α acids (leaf)		18g
Galaxy (leaf)		50g
Kohatu (leaf)		50g

Yeast

Wheat beer yeast	11–25g

Ancillary Materials

Add 45 minutes into the boil:	Irish Moss or Protafloc tablet	1tsp ¼
Auxiliary finings Isinglass	Add at end of fermentation	90ml 90ml
	Priming sugar per 500ml bottle	5.3g

Additional Ingredients

Mango puree	Add towards end of fermentation	1kg

- -

RECIPE 7.2: 4.3%ABV RASPBERRY SOUR

- Target volume = 25ltr
- Bitterness = 8BU
- Colour = 8EBC
- Final gravity = 1.009

Description:

Parameters		Process Parameters	
ABV (%)	4.3	Strike temperature	72°C
OG	1.043	Mash temperature	65°C
PG	1.009	Liquor to grist ratio	2.7
Bitterness (BU)	8	Liquor volume (ltr)	12
Colour (EBC)	8	Mash time (hours)	1
Mash efficiency (%)	80	Boil time (hours)	1
Hop efficiency (%)	35		
Volume (ltr)	25		
CO_2 (g/ltr)	5.5		

Ingredients:

	Specification	Amount
Water Treatment		Refer to
Alkalinity	Adjust in HLB	water
Calcium sulphate	Add to mash	treatment
Calcium chloride		table for IPA
Cereals and Adjuncts		
Pale malt	4EBC	3.6kg
Wheat malt	3.5EBC	900g
Hops		
Bittering: Magnum (leaf)	10% α acids	5g
Yeast		
American ale yeast	Sour culture	11–25g
Ancillary Materials		
Add 45 minutes into the boil:	Irish Moss or Protafloc tablet	1tsp ¼
Add at end of fermentation	Priming sugar per 500ml bottle	5.3g
Additional Ingredients		
Add 10 minutes before the end of boil or in fermentation	Raspberries	2kg

- -

RECIPE 7.3: 6%ABV HONEY BEER

- Target volume = 25ltr
- Bitterness = 30BU
- Colour = 20EBC
- Final gravity = 1.012

Description:
ParametersProcess Parameters

ABV (%)	6	Strike temperature	72°C
OG	1.058	Mash temperature	65°C
PG	1.012	Liquor to grist ratio	2.7
Bitterness (BU)	30	Liquor volume (ltr)	12
Colour (EBC)	20	Mash time (hours)	1
Mash efficiency (%)	80	Boil time (hours)	1
Hop efficiency (%)	35		
Volume (ltr)	25		
CO_2 (g/ltr)	4		

Ingredients:

	Specification	Amount
Water Treatment		Refer to
Alkalinity	Adjust in HLB	water
Calcium sulphate	Add to mash	treatment
Calcium chloride		table for IPA

Cereals and Adjuncts

Pale malt	4EBC	5.4kg
Crystal malt	140EBC	200g

Hops

Bittering: Magnum (leaf)	10% α acids	21g
First Gold (leaf)		75g

Yeast

British ale yeast	11g–25g

Ancillary Materials

Add 45 minutes	Irish Moss or	1tsp
into the boil:	Protafloc tablet	¼
Add at end of	Auxiliary finings	90ml
fermentation:	Isinglass	90ml
	Priming sugar	3.8g
	per 500ml bottle	

Additional Ingredients

Honey	Add in fermentation	450g

GLOSSARY OF BREWING TERMS

Acetaldehyde By-product of the production of ethanol by yeast, having a green apple flavour. The purpose of beer maturation is the removal of this flavour by yeast.

Acetic acid (vinegar) Acid produced by a variety of yeasts and bacteria.

Acid washing Procedure used to clean yeast of unwanted bacteria by incubating in a solution of acid at pH2.2 and at 4°C immediately before fermentation. Sensitive bacteria die during this process.

Adjuncts Additional extract material added to the mash or copper. Grain adjuncts such as maize, rice or wheat are added to the mash to allow malt enzymes to digest their starch. Syrup adjuncts are added to the copper.

Alcohol by Volume (ABV) Measure of the strength of a beer by the level of alcohol it contains as millilitres of alcohol per 100g of beer.

Alcohol by Weight (ABW) Measure of the strength of a beer by the weight of alcohol it contains as grams of alcohol per 100g of beer.

Ale Term for top-fermenting beers as opposed to bottom-fermenting lager beers. Historically, ale was used to indicate a beer without hops.

Aleurone layer Outer layer of cells surrounding the barley endosperm. These cells synthesize amylases.

Amino acid Twenty compounds that make up the building blocks of proteins.

α-Amylase In mashing, α-amylase digests internal bonds of amylose and amylopectin to release a range of sizes of simple sugars and larger dextrins.

β-Amylase In mashing, β-amylase digests amylose and amylopectin molecules by releasing maltose units from the non-reducing ends of the starch chains.

Amylopectin Starch compound composed of a branched chain of glucose molecules and digested by α-and β-amylase enzymes during mashing.

Amylose Starch compound, composed of linear chains of glucose molecules.

Anthocyanogens Phenolic compounds released from malt during mashing. They may contribute to the colour of beer as well as complexing with proteins and precipitating to cause haze.

Bacteria Microscopic organisms with limited cell structure and small size – less than 1μm in length. Bacteria like neutral acidity, but some species, particularly acetic- and lactic-acid bacteria, can grow in beer and produce spoilage flavours.

Barley Principal cereal grain used in brewing. Two species, *Hordeum vulgare* and *Hordeum distichon*, are most grown.

Barley wine Classic strong ale with an ABV between 6.5 and 11%.

Beer Alcoholic beverage produced by the fermentation of sugars from malt and other cereals. Generally containing between 3 and 10%ABV and with the flavours of malt and hops.

Beer stone Deposit of mineral and organic materials in the fermenter due to the precipitation of calcium salts and proteins.

Biotin Vitamin essential for the growth of brewing yeast.

Bitter   One of the predominant beers served in Britain, renowned for its balance of bitterness, malt and fruitiness. Brewed from pale and crystal malts with high hop additions, the beer is light or amber in colour and rich in hop aroma.

Bitterness   Beer flavour produced by the α acids from hops. These are isomerized by boiling and converted to the bitter iso-α acids. Bitterness levels are measured in IBU (International Bitterness Units). 1IBU = 1mg/l of iso-α acid.

Bottom fermentation   Beer fermented with a yeast that readily settles to the bottom of the fermenter, typically a lager yeast.

Brettanomyces   Genus of wild (non-brewing) yeast that produces acetic acid and various distinctive flavours, including butyric acid, caproic acid and capric esters. *Brettanomyces* yeasts are commonly used in sour Belgian beers.

Bright beer   Beer racked off its sediment of yeast into a fresh container for dispense. Such beer does not require settling and is served quickly.

Brown ale   Distinctive type of British beer characterized by a moderate bitterness and strong malt character.

Calcium oxalate   Insoluble salt precipitated from wort by boiling and over time during the fermentation. Will form crystals that may become embedded in beer stone, or remain suspended in the beer to cause a light haze.

Caramel   Material produced by the heating of sugars; it is added to beer to adjust or intensify colour and flavour.

Carbonation   Inclusion of carbon dioxide in beer to produce a fizz and effervescence.

Carrageenan   Seaweed extract used as finings to accelerate settlement of protein trub at the end of boiling and yeast after fermentation.

Cask-conditioned beer   *See* 'Real ale'.

Casks   Vessels for dispensing beer. Typical shape is cylindrical with a belly to keep settled yeast away from the tap. When stillaged, the top has a shive bung that is opened to allow air or gas into the cask. Beer is drawn from a tap inserted into the keystone bung in the side.

Co-humulone   Major species of α acid extracted from hops.

Cold break   Precipitated trub produced when beer cools. It is composed of lipids, proteins and tannins and a good cold break is important to minimize haze formation in the final beer.

Collagen   *See* 'Isinglass'.

Conditioning   Maturation of beer to produce the target balance of flavours, carbonation and clarification.

Copper (kettle)   Boiling vessel for wort.

Decoction mashing   Traditional continental mashing procedure.

Dextrins   Sugars composed of four and twenty glucose units bonded together. Dextrins are not fermented by brewing yeast and remain in the beer to give the impression of body and mouthfeel.

Diacetyl   *See* 'Vicinyl diketones'.

Dimethyl sulphide (DMS)   Distinctive flavour of beer with the character of cooked vegetables, cabbage, sweetcorn or Brussels sprouts.

Dissolved oxygen (DO$_2$)   Level of oxygen dissolved in wort or beer. Insignificant amounts are needed to oxidize sensitive flavour compounds to produce cardboard or papery flavours given time.

Dunkel beer   German dark lager.

Endosperm   Starch storage part of cereal grains.

Esters   Flavour compounds produced by the reaction between acids and alcohols such as banana, pear drop or red apple fruit flavours

Ethyl acetate   Ester produced by yeast metabolism during fermentation and maturation from the combination of acetate and ethanol and has a solvent-like flavour.

Extract mash   Production of wort using cereal extracts either as a liquid syrup or as a dried powder.

Fermentation   Dominant reaction of yeast metabolism, which produces ethanol and carbon dioxide from glucose. Energy is also produced and used by the cell for growth and multiplication.

Fermenter   Vessel used to ferment beer.

Ferulic acid   Phenolic compound released by malt and converted to spicy flavours such as vinyl guaiacol (the flavour of wheat beers) by wild yeast.

Filtration   Means of clarifying wort and beers by passage through a membrane with pores or convoluted layers of fibres or particles.

Finings Processing aids added to wort or beer to assist the flocculation and settlement of solid particles, particularly trub and yeast.

Flocculation Ability of yeasts to aggregate together and so float or settle rapidly. Flocculation is initiated towards the end of fermentation when sugar levels are low, and alcohol is high.

Foam Froth produced on the top of beer when dispensed. Composed of a mixture of protein, polysaccharides and isohumulones it forms a layer of liquid around gas bubbles released from the beer.

Fuggles Variety of hop developed in 1875 by Richard Fuggle, an important variety used in traditional British beers.

β-Glucan Polymer found in cereal grains and released by the malting and mashing processes into wort. It is a plant gum and will act to thicken wort and give body to beer, but also increase wort filtration time.

β-Glucanase Digestive enzyme present in cereal grains that digests β-glucan.

Glycogen Storage polysaccharide accumulated in yeast cells. Glycogen provides energy for the cells when they start fermentation after storage.

Grain mash Production of beer using cereal grains.

Gravity of worts and beer Measure of the density of wort and beer. Commonly measured by the buoyancy of a saccharometer calibrated for sugar solutions against a water density of 1.000 at 20°C. The starting or original gravity of a fermentation is termed the OG (Original Gravity) whilst the subsequent gravities are termed the PG (Present Gravity) or SG (Specific Gravity) or FG (Final Gravity).

Grist Total of dry goods added to the mash tun.

Gushing Violent release of gas and beer from a bottle.

Gypsum Calcium sulphate salt. Added to the grist to provide treatment of the liquor in the mash. Sulphates enhance bitterness.

Hallertau Traditional Eastern European hop commonly used in lager beers.

Haze Term used to describe light turbidity in worts and beers, usually due to the presence of protein-tannin particles, oxalic-acid crystals or microbial contamination.

Home brewing Non-commercial production of beer, usually at a home as a hobby for personal consumption.

Hop back Vessel used to retain hops as the wort drains from the copper.

Hop oils Volatile organic fraction of 300 compounds containing most of the aroma flavours of hops.

Hop resins Waxy materials extracted from hops holding the α and β acids.

Hops *Humulus lupulus*: major brewing ingredient added to boiling wort to produce bitterness and hop aroma.

Hot break Trub material precipitated by the boiling of wort. Consists of a mixture of lipids, proteins and tannins.

Hot Liquor Tank (HLT) Vessel used to heat liquor for the mash tun.

Humulone Major α acid extracted from hops; converted to bitter isohumulone by boiling.

Husk Outer layer of the malt grain used to filter wort in a mash tun.

India Pale Ale British beer developed as an export to overseas colonies and possessing strong bitterness to resist contamination during transit. Reputed as a high-alcohol beer with a pungent hop character.

Infusion mashing Traditional mashing process involving keeping the mash at a single temperature typically between 60 and 70°C.

Irish Moss Seaweed extract added to boiling wort to encourage precipitation of proteins at the end of the boil.

Isinglass Collagen extract from fish swim bladders, used as a fining aid to settle yeast in the maturation of beer and in cask-conditioned beer.

Keg Straight-sided pressure container for serving beer via a single-entry valve, with a central tube for exit of the beer and a surrounding collar for entry of pressurized gas to push the beer out.

Lactic acid Acid produced by a variety of yeasts and bacteria. Major spoilage flavour, having a yogurt-like aroma and taste.

Lactobacillus One of the predominant groups of lactic-acid bacteria that produces lactic acid.

Lager   Term for bottom-fermented beers, although traditionally used to designate beers matured for extended periods at cold temperature. Lager beers today are light in colour, have some DMS aroma and are less bitter in taste.

Lambic ales   Traditional beer of Belgium spontaneously fermented with a complex mixture of moulds, wild yeast and bacteria to produce a sour, cider-like flavour.

Liquor   Brewing terminology for brewing water.

Lupulone   Spicy flavoured component of hop oil.

Malt   Brewing ingredient providing sugars for yeast fermentation. Usually derived from barley, although other grains such as wheat, oats and rye may also be malted.

Malting   Process of making malt using three phases of steeping, germination and kilning.

Maltose   Major wort disaccharide sugar composed of two glucose molecules.

Maltotriose   Major wort disaccharide sugar composed of three glucose molecules.

Mashing   First major stage in the brewing process, in which malt and liquor are mixed and left to incubate at set temperature(s). Starch is converted to simple sugars and compounds are provided from the malt to enrich the wort.

Melanoidins   Darkly pigmented compounds produced by the combination of simple sugars and amino acids. This reaction mostly occurs during wort boiling.

Mercaptans   Distinctive flavour compounds with the aroma of skunk. Produced by light reacting with hop compounds.

Microbiology   Study of living organisms too small to be visible to the naked eye.

Mild ale   Distinctive British beer with low hop, brewed with dark malts to give a caramel and liquorice character and solid body.

Milling   Milling crushes grains before mashing and so exposes the internal contents to the mash liquor and enhances dissolving and digestion by malt enzymes.

Oats   Ancillary grain used in some beers to give a malty character and smooth mouthfeel.

Old ale   Traditional British beer with high alcohol levels and rich, complex flavours.

Oxalic acid   Organic acid released into wort from barley and other grains. Can complex with calcium to produce precipitated crystals of calcium oxalate.

Paraflow   Paraflow heat exchangers are used to cool wort. They are constructed of a series of stainless-steel parallel plates with wort running across one side and chilled water running across the other.

Pediococcus   Coccus variety of lactic-acid bacteria with the ability to produce high levels of lactic acid and so spoil wort and beer.

Permanently soluble nitrogen   Fraction of protein compounds staying after precipitation in the boil. These proteins will contribute to head formation and mouthfeel of beer.

pH   Scale to show the acidity or alkalinity of a solution. The scale is logarithmical and goes from 1 (acidic) to 14 (alkaline).

Pilsner   Classic continental beer using Saaz or Hallertau hops to provide a distinctive flowery aroma. The beer is a golden and aromatic lager with a dry finish.

Pitching   Term used by brewers for the addition of yeast to wort.

Plato (degrees of measurement)   Plato is the strength to the concentration of sugar in solution. 1° Plato is equivalent to 1g of sucrose dissolved in water. A wort of 1.040° will be 10° Plato.

Porter   British beer characterized by a balance of malt, roast, hop, bitterness, fruit and spicy flavours.

Priming sugar   Sugars added to beer after fermentation to restart yeast activity and fermentation. Important in some cask ales and bottle-conditioned beers where a secondary fermentation is necessary to produce additional carbonation.

Protein   Category of biomolecules comprised of a complex of different amino acids.

Proteolytic enzymes   Enzymes found in malt that digest proteins into polypeptides (small proteins) and amino acids.

Real ale   Term used for cask-conditioned ale – beer that undergoes a secondary conditioning after the primary fermentation. This conditioning typically takes place in a cask or bottle that contains live yeast.

Saccharometer or hydrometer   Instrument for measuring the density of sugar in a liquid at 20°C. It can be used to indicate the strength of a beer.

Saccharomyces   Genus of yeast particularly adapted to fermentation of strong sugar solutions, so producing high levels of alcohol. *Saccharomyces cerevisiae* is the traditional brewing yeast.

Skimming   Removal of yeast from the top of a fermentation vessel at the end of the fermentation process.

Slack malt   Malt that has absorbed water and become soft and stale.

Sparging   Washing of grains using liquor at about 77°C after mashing, to remove residual sugars and maximize extract.

Spent grains   Solids remaining at the end of sparging in the mash tun.

Starch   Major storage polysaccharide in barley. A glucose polymer having two molecular species – the linear polymer amylase (around 20%) and the branched polymer amylopectin (around 80%).

Stout   British beer developed as a strong version of Porter. Characterized by a strong roast flavour due to the use of roast barley grains, stout was initially a high-alcohol beer with a rich aroma and strong burnt taste.

Strike temperature   Temperature of the brewing liquor added to the mash.

Sucrose   Disaccharide composed of glucose and fructose.

Sunstruck beer   *See* 'Mercaptans'.

Temperature-programmed mashing   Mashing regime that involves a stepped increase in temperature. Typical steps involve temperature stands at 35–40°C for digestion of β-glucans, at 50°C for digestion of proteins, at 65°C for digestion of starch and a final rise to 76°C to stop all enzyme activity.

Top fermenting yeast   Yeasts rise to the top of the beer during fermentation. These yeasts stay on the surface as a yeast head and may be skimmed for repitching in a future brew.

Trub   Precipitated proteins, tannins and lipids produced in hot wort during boiling and in cold wort after collection in the fermenter.

Ullage   Residual content in a tank or cask.

Underback   Vessel taking the wort from the mash tun at an even rate, so preventing compaction of the mash bed.

Unitank   Fermentation vessel, which may also be used for conditioning.

Viability   Proportion of live cells in a sample of yeast. Commonly tested using methylene blue stain.

Vicinyl Diketones (VDK)   Produced during fermentation by yeast metabolism. The common VDK is diacetyl, which has a very strong butterscotch flavour at low concentrations. Diacetyl levels rise towards the end of fermentation, but are then reduced by yeast to produce the less flavoursome 2,3-butanediol.

Water treatments   Treatments to adjust and control the acidity of the mash, usually by the addition of acid to neutralize the bicarbonate salts and by addition of calcium salts to enhance the release of acid from phytate. Typical treatments may be to add sulphuric acid to the hot liquor, followed by a mixture of calcium sulphate and calcium chloride to the mash.

Whirlpool   Vessel to capture the wort from the kettle and produce a spinning motion so that particles gravitate to a central sump and thus clarify the wort. The motion may arise from a tangential entry or by an external pump.

Wild yeasts   Non-brewing yeasts are termed wild. *Pichia*, *Brettanomyces* or *Hansenula* can produce distinctive flavours, as well as turbidity.

Wort   Sugar solution produced by the mashing process. Wort also contains proteins, amino acids, phenols, vitamins and minerals and is an excellent medium for the growth of microorganisms.

Yeast   *See* 'Saccharomyces'.

Zymomonas   Bacterial contaminant of beer. *Zymomonas mobilis* is the major species found and produces very distinctive vegetal off flavours, as well as some lactic acid.

APPENDICES

APPENDIX I HAMMOND'S BREWERY, 1903 XXXX RECIPE

COMMENTARY

This recipe is transcribed from the original sheet in the Bass Museum of Brewing and shows details of the different aspects of an Edwardian brew of XXXX strong ale on 29 May 1903. The top of the recipe sheet left lists the malts and sugars added in units of quarters and calculates the total input in brewer's pounds.

Below these is the hop list, with two UK and one continental supply. 'MK' indicates mid-Kent and 'Sx' Sussex, but the varieties are not known. The times noted,

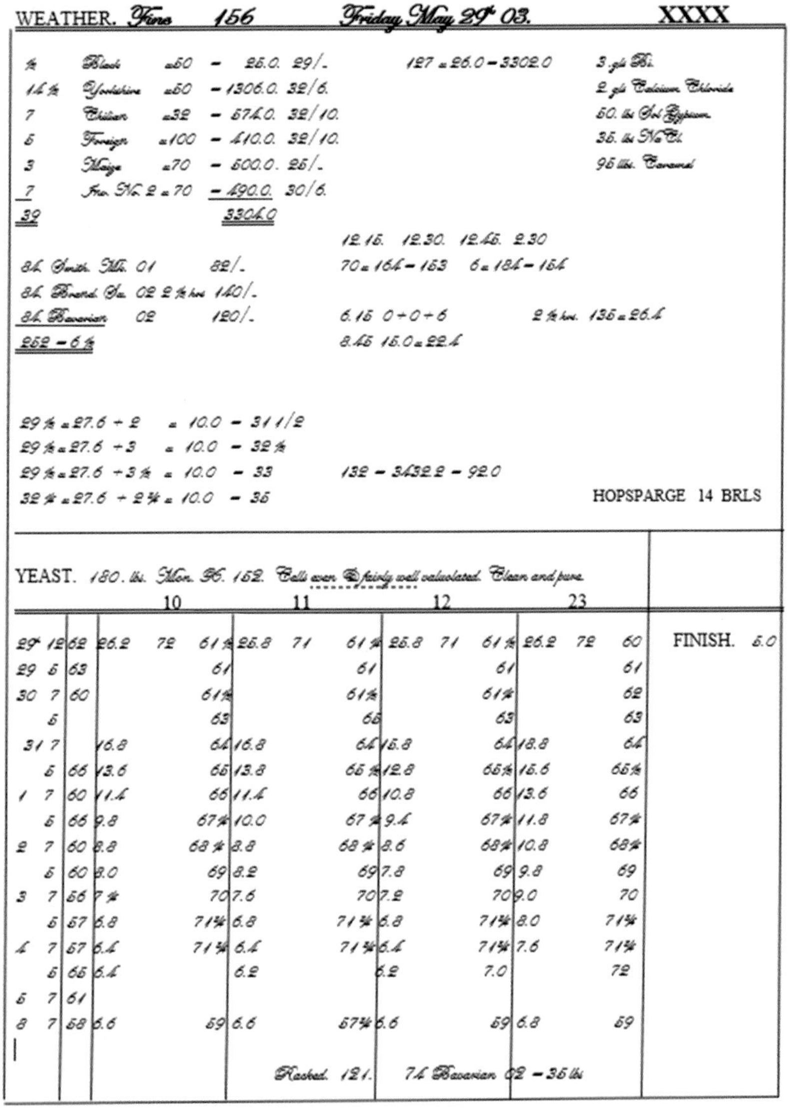

WEATHER. Fine 156 Friday May 29th 03. XXXX

½ Black =50 – 25.0. 29/-
14½ Yorkshire =50 – 1306.0. 32/6.
7 Chilian =32 – 574.0. 32/10.
5 Foreign =100 – 410.0. 32/10.
3 Maize =70 – 500.0. 25/-
7 Inv. No. 2 = 70 – 490.0. 30/6.
39 3304.0

127 = 26.0 – 3302.0

3 gls Bi.
2 gls Calcium Chloride
50. lbs Sol Gypsum
35. lbs NaCl
95 lbs. Caramel

84 Smith MK 01 82/-
84 Brand Sx 02 2½ hrs 140/-
84 Bavarian 02 120/-
252 – 6½

12.15. 12.30. 12.45. 2.30
70 = 164 – 153 6 = 184 – 154
6.15 0 + 0 + 6 2½ hrs. 135 = 26.4
8.45 15.0 = 22.4

29½ = 27.6 + 2 = 10.0 – 31 1/2
29½ = 27.6 + 3 = 10.0 – 32½
29½ = 27.6 + 3½ = 10.0 – 33 132 – 3432.2 – 92.0
32¼ = 27.6 + 2¾ = 10.0 – 35

HOPSPARGE 14 BRLS

YEAST. 180. lbs. Mon. 96. 152. Cells even & fairly well calculated. Clean and pure

			10			11			12			23			
29th	12	62	26.2	72	61½	25.8	71	61½	25.8	71	61½	26.2	72	60	FINISH. 5.0
29	5	63			61			61			61			61	
30	7	60			61½			61½			61½			62	
	5				63			65			63			63	
31	7		16.8		64	16.8		64	15.8		64	18.8		64	
	5	66	13.6		65	13.8		65½	12.8		65½	15.6		65½	
1	7	60	11.4		66	11.4		66	10.8		66	13.6		66	
	5	66	9.8		67½	10.0		67½	9.4		67½	11.8		67½	
2	7	60	8.8		68½	8.8		68½	8.6		68½	10.8		68½	
	5	60	8.0		69	8.2		69	7.8		69	9.8		69	
3	7	56	7½		70	7.6		70	7.2		70	9.0		70	
	5	57	6.8		71¼	6.8		71¼	6.8		71¼	8.0		71¼	
4	7	57	6.4		71¼	6.4		71¼	6.4		71¼	7.6		71¼	
	5	65	6.4			6.2			6.2		7.0			72	
5	7	61													
8	7	58	6.6		59	6.6		57¾	6.6		59	6.8		59	

Racked. 121. 74 Bavarian 02 – 35 lbs

Fig. A1 Hammond's Brewery XXXX recipe, 29 May 1903.

12.15, 12.30, 12.45 and 2.30, suggest points of hop addition, but proportions at each are not stated.

The top right shows the salt additions and the bottom left a calculation of total volume and extract collected to allow duty to be calculated.

The yeast addition is from the brew of X beer on Monday; gyle 143 and microscopic observation indicates the condition to be satisfactory.

Fermentation was conducted in four vessels, 10, 11, 12 and 23, and progress indicated by temperatures measured in Fahrenheit and gravity in brewer's pounds, the latter decreasing from 26 to 6.6 in the measurements on 8 June, but stated as 5.0 in final attenuation, presumably determined at a later date.

APPENDIX II
F-FACTOR TABLE

F-factor table for calculating ABV from specific gravity and specific gravity from ABV.

Specific Gravity	Alcohol %	F-Factor
26.2–36.0	3.3–4.6	0.129
36.1–46.5	4.6–6.0	0.130
46.6–57.1	6.0–7.5	0.131
57.2–67.9	7.5–9.0	0.132

For example:

- to determine the alcohol in a beer that has a fall in gravity from 1.045 to 1.008 (37°) ABV = 37 × 0.129 = 4.8%
- to determine the fall in gravity to produce a beer of 5.2%ABV, divide the ABV by the F- factor, that is, 5.2/0.13 = 40.

APPENDIX III
STORAGE OF RAW MATERIALS

Storage of materials, as well as whether they can be used beyond their best-before date, is always a concern for the home brewer.

Malt has two enemies. One is moisture, while the other is pests, namely rodents and insects. The simple solution to both is to store malt sealed in a cool, dry environment. If storing in an outhouse or garage, it is best kept off the ground in a pest-proof container. Otherwise, it will be temptation for rodents looking for an easy dinner. Certainly, clean up spillages. Keep all containers tightly sealed to prevent moisture ingress, as this may allow fungal growth, which can produce deadly aflatoxins. Damp malt is known as slack malt. So, look out for any green contamination and discard the malt into the rubbish bin. Never feed to animals. Can you use malt beyond its best-before date? If stored correctly, it should be okay to use. Treat salts, sugars and adjuncts like malt.

Hops are prone to oxidation and if stored in open packets at room temperature will produce a cheesy smell akin to stale socks. You do not want such a smell in your beer! It is best to store hops in the freezer, if acceptable to others in the house. Both unopened and opened hops will keep well beyond their best-before date in this frozen condition. Open hop packets should be tightly resealed, with as much air expelled as possible. Bulldog clips are perfect for this. Failing access to a freezer, keep hops as cool as possible and always reseal the packets. To avoid using spoilt hops, always smell them prior to use.

Yeast is a living organism, even if bought in a dried format. So, store yeast in a refrigerator and never in the freezer. Like hops, reseal the packet, expelling all air. Liquid yeast should be stored at 3–4°C in a clean container, ideally in the refrigerator. Yeast may continue fermentation using residual sugars and generate CO_2. It is best to have a loose-fitting lid or pressure-relief valve and keep the yeast container in a drip tray. Any spillages of yeast will be time-consuming to clean up, so the drip tray aids towards a quicker clean-up and more stress-free life.

Dried yeast can be used beyond its best-before date, but beware of a sluggish start to fermentation and have a new yeast as a back-up in case of this issue. Liquid yeast must be used as quickly as possible and never stored for more than a week.

If using Isinglass or auxiliary finings, these should be kept in the refrigerator as they will denature with time. If you must use finings beyond their best-before date, test their potency using a small-scale finings test. This is simply taking the beer you wish to fine and adding pro rata the finings you wish to use, then observing the results. If the beer clarifies within an hour, the finings are still fit for purpose.

APPENDIX IV
HOME-BREW
SUPPLIERS

A changing range of suppliers provides equipment and materials for home brewing. Many of these can be found on the internet today, although some shops do exist. A few national hardware shops also provide off-the-shelf kits and materials.

Raw materials can be obtained from standard brewing suppliers for malt and hops, although you may have to purchase a minimum order such as a 25kg sack of malt. The major suppliers of these are listed below, although other companies may act as agents.

MALT

Crisp Maltings: https://crispmalt.com/
Tel: +44 (0)1328 829 391
Email: hello@crispmalt.com

Fawcett & Sons Ltd: www.fawcett-maltsters.co.uk/malts.html
Tel: +44 (0)1977 552460
Email: sales@fawcett-maltsters.co.uk

Muntons: www.muntons.com/
Dedicated Muntons home-brew stockists: www.muntons.com/stockists/

Simpsons Malt: www.simpsonsmalt.co.uk
Tel: +44 (0)1289 330033
Email: info@simpsonsmalt.co.uk

Warminster Maltings Ltd: www.warminster-malt.co.uk
Tel: +44 (0)1985 212014
Email: info@warminster-malt.co.uk

HOPS

Brewers Select: www.brewersselect.co.uk
Tel +44 (0)1733 889100
Email: sales@brewersselect.co.uk

Brook House Hops: www.brookhousehops.com
Tel: +44 (0)1885 562462
Email: hops@brookhousehops.com

Charles Faram: www.wellhopped.com
Tel +44 (0)1905 830734
Email: sales@charlesfaram.co.uk

Steiner Hops Ltd: www.hopsteiner.com/uk
Tel +44(0)1992 572331
Email: enquiries@hopsteiner.co.uk

YEAST

Lallemand UK: www.abvickers.com
Tel: +44 (0)1283 563268
Email: ab_vickers@lallemand.com

National Collection of Yeast Cultures (NCYC): www.ncyc.co.uk
Tel +44 (0)1603 255274
Email: ncyc@ncyc.co.uk

APPENDIX V
HOME-BREW CLUBS
AND ASSOCIATIONS

HOME-BREW CLUBS

An extensive network of home-brew associations and clubs exists across the UK. Some are local and informal, while others are part of national organizations.

The Homebrewers Association is an international body based in America, but collating home-brew groups in forty-five countries, as well as providing a wealth of supporting material and coordinating competition events. The Association hosts a tasting qualification incorporating an on-line examination and a monthly home-brewing magazine, *Zymurgy*. www.homebrewersassociation.org

The London Amateur Brewers provides for meetings and events in London and has an extensive portfolio of recipes and advice. The LAB hosts presentations from industry specialists and has many examples of members developing commercial breweries. https://londonamateurbrewers.co.uk

The Craft Brewing Association is a national UK body providing amateur support and activities, including conferences and competitions. www.craftbrewing.org.uk

Brew Con organizes a home-brewing conference and expo in London in November every year, providing extensive participation of suppliers, talks and collaborations. The Brew Con website hosts an extensive list of local UK beer clubs at www.brew-con.co.uk/brew-clubs-of-britain.

PROFESSIONAL INDUSTRY BODIES

The brewing industry has some long-established professional bodies that serve as representative of the industry, as well as providing support for breweries and their brewers. Training is a major focus of the 125-year-old Institute of Brewing & Distilling, alongside providing technical advice and professional examinations. www.ibd.org.uk/home/

The Society of Independent Brewers is a professional body representing smaller breweries, with a strong emphasis on providing business support, including bulk purchase and a sales distribution service. An annual exposition trade show, BeerX, is a major UK gathering of suppliers and lecturers. www.siba.co.uk.

The London Brewers Alliance is a more local collective of breweries in the London area coordinating events and collaborations. www.londonbrewers.org.

The Brewers Association is a major professional body for American brewing, with extensive activities and materials to support training and advice to the industry. An extensive bookshop provides informative publications suitable for both amateur and commercial brewers. The association is active in lobbying for the industry, organizing annual events and major international competitions. www.brewersassociation.org.

Although a consumer organization rather than an industry body, the Campaign for Real Ale does have support for home brewing and provides some useful literature on beer styles. www.camra.org.uk

OTHER SUPPORT

The Brewery History Society www.breweryhistory.com has an extensive archive of brewery artifacts and documents. A regular journal reports studies in brewery history and recent projects into all aspects of breweries, brewing technology, beer styles and drinking culture.

The Brewers Journal www.brewersjournal.info publishes a monthly magazine for the brewing trade, but also hosts a major annual conference, the Brewers Congress, in December, featuring events and a trade show.

Zymurgy is a monthly home-brewing magazine produced by the American Home Brewers Association, carrying a wide range of information relevant to techniques, recipes and commentary. An increasingly broad range of fermentation topics addresses additional interests and complements substantial reports on home-brewing competitions and achievements.
www.homebrewersassociation.org/zymurgy-magazine

An increasing number of home-brew suppliers provide information and support on their websites. These provide information on products, but also best practice and background theory. New techniques and equipment are often featured and commentary boards are available to view experience and feedback.

INDEX